To Sandy

Happy

I think you probably don't
have to read this - because
you already delight God
with your wonderful bold
witness ⌐

Maybe this will help
with your Bible Study.

I am proud to be your friend,
Love, Laurie

$\mathscr{D}$elighting
God

The Secret to Making the Father's Heart Leap

"It's the child he loves that GOD corrects; a father's delight is behind all this" (Proverbs 3:12, MSG).

VICTORIA BROOKS

NAVPRESS

Bringing Truth to Life
P.O. Box 35001, Colorado Springs, Colorado 80935

OUR GUARANTEE TO YOU

We believe so strongly in the message of our books that we are making this quality guarantee to you. If for any reason you are disappointed with the content of this book, return the title page to us with your name and address and we will refund to you the list price of the book. To help us serve you better, please briefly describe why you were disappointed. Mail your refund request to: NavPress, P.O. Box 35002, Colorado Springs, CO 80935.

The Navigators is an international Christian organization. Our mission is to reach, disciple, and equip people to know Christ and to make Him known through successive generations. We envision multitudes of diverse people in the United States and every other nation who have a passionate love for Christ, live a lifestyle of sharing Christ's love, and multiply spiritual laborers among those without Christ.

NavPress is the publishing ministry of The Navigators. NavPress publications help believers learn biblical truth and apply what they learn to their lives and ministries. Our mission is to stimulate spiritual formation among our readers.

ISBN 1-57683-372-0

Cover design by Jennifer Mahalik
Cover illustration Kandinsky/Planet Art
Creative Team: Don Simpson, Amy Spencer, Glynese Northam

Some of the anecdotal illustrations in this book are true to life and are included with the permission of the persons involved. All other illustrations are composites of real situations, and any resemblance to people living or dead is coincidental.

Unless otherwise identified, all Scripture quotations in this publication are taken from the *New American Standard Bible* (NASB), © The Lockman Foundation 1960, 1962, 1963, 1968, 1971, 1972, 1973, 1975, 1977. Other versions used are the HOLY BIBLE: NEW INTERNATIONAL VERSION® (NIV®), Copyright © 1973, 1978, 1984 by International Bible Society, used by permission of Zondervan Publishing House, all rights reserved; the *Holy Bible, New Living Translation*, (NLT) copyright © 1996. Used by permission of Tyndale House Publishers, Inc., Wheaton, Illinois 60189. All rights reserved; the *Amplified New Testament* (AMP), © The Lockman Foundation 1954, 1958; *The Message: New Testament with Psalms and Proverbs* (MSG) by Eugene H. Peterson, copyright © 1993, 1994, 1995, used by permission of NavPress Publishing Group; and the *King James Version* (KJV).

Portions of this book have been previously published under the title *Ministering to God, The Reach of the Heart.*

Brooks, Victoria, 1953-
  Delighting God : the secret to making the Father's heart leap /
Victoria Brooks.
    p. cm.
Includes bibliographical references.
  ISBN 1-57683-372-0
  1. Christian life. I. Title.
  BV4501.3 .B755 2003
  248.4--dc21
                                    2002012209
Printed in the United States of America
1 2 3 4 5 6 7 8 9 10 / 07 06 05 04 03

FOR A FREE CATALOG OF
NAVPRESS BOOKS & BIBLE STUDIES,
CALL 1-800-366-7788 (USA)
OR 1-416-499-4615 (CANADA)

This book is lovingly dedicated to my parents,

Dick and Jody Larson:

To Dad, whose godly character as a
father has consistently revealed to me
the fatherly character of God

To Mom, whose feisty Scottish soul
responds to God with genuine fervor
and childlike faith

CONTENTS

ACKNOWLEDGMENTS

*T*HIS BOOK IS the product of many people's patience and prayer—particularly that of my husband, Mike. His wisdom, encouragement, and late-night talks (worked into an overloaded schedule) have sustained me. Mike, the guilelessness and grace with which you face life's toughest problems have given my heart safe harbor. You are the strongest man I know. I am the luckiest woman I know.

With joy and gratitude I also thank . . .
Nathan, Jordan, and Zion, who have helped me with this message in hundreds of hidden ways and whose energy, antics, and creativity have kept me motivated to finish before they have to shop and cook again. I'm proud of you, my sons. May you always walk worthy of your high calling in Christ, for *He* is worthy.

Kristie Dolan, who committed herself to prayer on behalf of this book even before the first chapter had taken shape. Few people realize what it cost you to remain faithful in prayer for this project. This message will always carry the brand of your passionate heart.

Francis and Denise Frangipane, whose years of friendship, encouragement, and pastoral leadership have formed the spiritual incubator within which these thoughts have matured and grown strong. Thank you.

Dick and Linda Swenson, whose reading of the original book led them to recommend it to their editor at NavPress.

Thank you both for your early encouragement and support of this message.

To Don Simpson and Amy Spencer at NavPress: Don, your commitment to this book and its message has touched my heart. Without your wisdom, grace, and dedication, it would not have been accomplished. God has seen the "extra" you gave and I'm sure is as blessed as I am. Thank you, friend. Amy, your feisty, poetic, paper-clip-spitting soul gave me a boost when I needed it. Thanks for your passion and excellence.

To my cousin, Eric Carlson—because you have *always* loved The Music.

To our friends on the River of Life leadership team and in our Home Group and Joy Group for your prayer support; to Meg Diehl, Kevin Dwyer and Alan Pieratt for reviewing the manuscript; to Deb Klopp, Bev Pospisil, Lila Nelson, and Joe and Bonnie Gates for specific feedback; and to Capi Mabie, Marvin and Joia Eales, Deb Polk, Sandy Boller, Jennifer Owens, Cindy Young, Susan Aulwes, Rick and Kristi Casteel, Dorothy Gouldin, and Brian and Robin Perry for your practical help and prayer. Thanks, everybody.

It is with fresh gratitude that I remember those who helped me with portions of this book previously published under the title *Ministering to God: The Reach of the Heart*: To Scott Larson and Meg Diehl, my much-loved brother and sister, for their early encouragement and individual expertise in bringing the manuscript to print; to my amazing friend, Lila Nelson, who gave painstaking attention to detail with the text, in both substance and layout; and to Billie Barker, for her special ability to find and kill clutter words—without sacrificing intent. I also remember with love the family and friends in Wheaton, Illinois; St. Louis, Missouri; and North Port, Florida; who read portions of the early manuscript and offered valuable suggestions.

Acknowledgments

Finally, and most importantly, I give grateful, loving praise to my God and King, Jesus Christ. Thank you, Lord, for filling first my heart and then my head, with the truths contained in these pages.

Part One

THE FURNACE
OF FELLOWSHIP

Now Mount Sinai was all in smoke because the LORD descended upon it in fire; and its smoke ascended like the smoke of a furnace, and the whole mountain quaked violently.

Exodus 19:18

One

THE QUEST

An experienced gardener knows a variety of ways to prepare the earth and plant a seed. So does God. Usually His trowel is quick, smooth, and not too disruptive. On rare occasions He arrives with shovel and hoe, ready to greatly trouble the tight soil of our souls. With dagger thrusts He works the earth, preparing it for a single, precious, deep-seated seed.

CHICAGO TRAFFIC was normal for 5:30 P.M. I sat staring at the bumper in front of me, listening to the muffled sounds of the freeway. I was staring and listening, but like every other trip to and from work that year, I saw and heard more of the traffic in my head than outside my car. Regardless of how slowly the car was creeping along, my brain was always speeding. Total standstills on the Eisenhower Expressway were just renewed opportunities for my mind to race forward, change lanes, dodge in and out, and cut off slower-moving thoughts. This day was the same as every other. My mind kept racing, searching. Over and over the same words collided within me: "There must be more. There has to be more. . . . "

Actually, I was headed directly into what most twenty-year-olds consider "more." I was engaged to be married. He was great, and we were sure we would be happy. He talked; I listened. I talked; he listened. It was a good relationship. So

15

why was House of Brides the last place I wanted to pass on my way home at night? What was this fear that gripped me every time I thought about wedding cakes and diamonds, white lace and flowers?

Certainly, marriage to a fine Christian man would be meaningful enough to fill this widening gap in my gut. Surely, the questions in my head would be answered, in time, if I just kept moving forward into life's inevitables. Unaware that four more years would pass before I met the man who was to become my husband, I tried to enter wholeheartedly into the season of this engagement. I worked at being carefree and in love, but like everything else that had hit my heart since my return from college, my turmoil increased.

A confusing, gripping pain lodged deep down where my happiness should have been. Like a high-class burglary gone bad, it tore through every locked door, unbolting and unhinging as it went. I was dismantled, torn apart inside. Accompanying the pain were all the hallmarks of an existential crisis. Overwhelmed by futility and loss, I felt the anguish of profound separation from God—suddenly, unexpectedly—with no understanding of why.

A fog of anxiety and fear settled over everything. Every decision I made I countered with indecision; every forward movement found me further removed from the things that had always given shape and meaning to my life.

Without warning, I was trapped in the book of Ecclesiastes. All was vanity. I found myself absentmindedly repeating the words again and again: "There must be more. Surely we were born for something more." More than waking in order to work, working in order to eat, eating and sleeping in order to wake and work again. More than graduating to have a career, marrying to have children so they could eventually graduate, work, marry, and have children of their own. The cycle of survival wasn't enough.

My pastor and a counselor were in strong agreement with each other: suicide was no solution. I wasn't so sure. Somehow, in a strange, twisted way, it seemed like the honest thing to do. I was already dying inside, and I felt there should be consistency between my thoughts and actions. Why go on with plans for living and loving when life and love weren't real anymore?

I felt completely cut off from God and all His purposes. My body moved by habit through the days and duties of two jobs, fiancé, family, friends, roommates, and church. My heart was in shock; my mind was at war.

Every time the car door closed and the engine started, I would begin the search all over again. Those forty-five minutes of solitude twice a day were my chance to look for clues. Relentlessly, my mind traveled back six months to June 1974, when my inner battle had begun. What had happened? What had set off this incredible heart-darkness? Why could I no longer sense God's presence or hear His voice? What had caused such a sudden decline in my otherwise "normal Christian life"?

Theoretically, if I could find the road into this mess, I could travel back out. But there was nothing. There were no breadcrumbs to follow and no memory of any one thing that led me so far from home. Nothing situational or circumstantial could be reversed to make it all better. I was stuck. As if a switch had been flipped, I was suddenly asking questions I couldn't answer. They were classic: "What is the purpose of my life?" "Why do I exist?" "For what reason have I been created?"

Tradition has it that everyone who grew up in the era of Woodstock and Janis Joplin eventually asks these questions, but I'd hoped to escape. I was a Christian, and it seemed that somewhere in the process of getting to know Jesus I would have answered these questions.

This, then, was the crux of the crisis. I already knew Jesus as my Lord and Savior . . . what more could there be? My faith told me He was sufficient. In high school, I'd been a "Jesus freak," not a flower child. I was born on the mission field, raised in a Christian home, and surrounded by the things of the church since I was very young. Most important, I hadn't merely inherited my faith in God. I had searched and struggled, scrapped and clawed my way to a living walk with Him. My parents didn't just talk about God's sovereignty; they believed in it and actively entrusted their children to His care. They knew that the four of us had to find our own way, so they set up a loving, faith-filled, Scripture-padded home and let us fight it out for ourselves.

Over supper, we would talk long and hard about the things of God. Then, too, there was enough rest from human voices for us to hear Him speak. Our home was a perfect greenhouse for all the vegetation of my early growth. Seasons came and went in this place of nurture, until my roots showed beneath the pot and I was transplanted to something bigger: college.

At the end of my first year, I returned home to work for more money to go back. At least that was the plan before this drought hit. Instead I was suddenly blistered and bone dry. Every path laid out in front of me seemed outdated, obsolete. I didn't need more political science; I needed to know why I was alive. I didn't want to watch lab rats emerge from a maze; I wanted to find a way out of *this* maze, my maze.

Sitting in a dorm hallway in my pink bathrobe and fuzzy slippers giggling over fistfuls of midnight popcorn suddenly seemed incongruous, absurd. Marriage, on the other hand, struck me as far too weighty, too heavy to be carried by this shell of a self. Every future plan faded.

One thing, however, did still burn in me—I wanted to hear God's voice again. This was not some sentimental longing for the "old days." This was survival. Nostalgia had wearied and wandered off months ago. This was the ragged remains of a famished heart searching for its Father. But He was silent.

It was a strange way for Him to loosen the deep, hardened soil of my heart, but it worked. I was desperate. I began to ask people, all sorts of people, why they thought they were alive. Exposing my struggle was more difficult than I had expected. Contriving ways to swing every conversation into deep discussion felt self-serving and awkward. I was shy about the nature of my need and contemplated softening my questions just to avoid exposure. But pride is a poor companion, and I was lonely, so I kept them pointed and stark: "Why do you think you exist? For what purpose are you alive?"

As I quizzed one person after another over the following few weeks, one thing became increasingly clear: this was an almost universal struggle. These questions were hard for all of us. In fact, as people struggled to respond, the questions always shifted and blurred: "Oh, you mean, what are my *goals?*"

This was easier; we all had goals. For some, it was as simple as wanting to retire and see the grandchildren more often. For others, career and travel plans were the focus. The tenderhearted altruists just wanted everyone in the world to be happy. We all passionately desired that there be an end to hunger and war.

For fellow Christians, the answer seemed to be evangelism. They desperately wanted everyone to hear about Jesus. I agreed. This was no minor objective, but somehow it didn't seem to be the true end to the road of inquiry I was traveling. I still sensed there was "more."

Having long since lost my ability to see the road, I groped along, blind to any real progress I might have been making. Thick fog continued to blanket everything around me, and I fought to find my way back to some familiar crossroad. I was so disoriented and confused during those days that now, years later, only one clear recollection remains with me. As I listened to the ultimate of each person's goals, a small light began to glimmer.

"Suppose you're retired and can see the grandkids every day," I would ask. "Now, why do you exist?" Or, "Suppose you've traveled and seen the world and have a wonderful career; in fact, let's just imagine that all war has ceased, famine has ended, and everyone is completely healthy and happy. All human need has been met. Now, why are you alive?" To the Christians I would say, "Suppose that somehow the household of faith is complete. Everyone who wants to know Jesus now does. Let's pretend there is no one left to evangelize. Now . . . why do you exist?"

For those not struggling with a deep crisis like I was, these discussions probably led to more confusion than clarity. But for me, the slender shaft of light slowly grew broader. Just by the silence that met these questions, my hunch was confirmed. Of course we had nothing to say! Of course we were silent as we grappled with eternity—we remained in the grip of all things temporal. What was there to say? Could those things we were most sure of, those measurable, quantifiable things that defined our days, ever really be enough to answer the heart's call for more? Could earthly activity, however noble or engrossing, be the only reason for which we had been summoned to this great green foyer called life?

Of course there was more! There had to be. We, who were created in God's image, eternal by nature, could surely expect some task that was also eternal to engage our passion and energy. We had to have been marked with a higher mandate than personal problem solving and global peacemaking. Certainly we were born for more than fruitful function here on earth, more even than fruitful evangelism. We had been brought into existence for something much greater than I yet understood, but I sensed its nearness, and that awareness was enough to keep me going.

ONE BRIGHT MORNING in the fall of 1975, it was over. As suddenly as I had gotten lost fifteen months before, I found my way back. I had my answer. It came, surprisingly, in the familiar formality of the Westminster Shorter Catechism of Faith:

> The chief end of man is to glorify God and enjoy
> Him forever.[1]

Without warning, these steady words took on fire and life beyond anything syllables and script could contain. No longer was this simply a timeworn Presbyterian motto. Never again would these words be just passive print on a yellowing page. They became my lifeline and my link with everything that had meaning and substance. After so many months of agonizing silence, they became the conveyor of that voice I most wanted to hear:

> *I am your reason for being, child — I am your "more." It is*
> *the King of the Kingdom that is your true end.*
>   *This season of correction has been hard, Child, I know.*
>   *You've been wounded by Me — left long in a far country*
> *and now I seem unpredictable and unloving.*

You thought you were alone, but I've never been more near.

You thought I was angry—but I've never loved you better.

I withdrew My felt presence so your hunger for Me would grow strong again, but

I never let you fall from My arms.

It was My love that was drawing you,

bending you back toward truth—toward Me.

Do you have any understanding of how far away you wandered?

Do you know how often you let the pain of this planet take your eyes from Me—your heart from Me?

It wasn't trust that drove you forward; it was fear. It wasn't fellowship with Me that sent you running so far ahead, so mindful of the needs,

so relentless in applying remedies.

For which of My many mercies do you seek to educate Me in compassion?

Is My love less ardent, less eager than your own? Is My beloved world more precious to you than My beloved Son was to Me?

No.

I am the One who emptied heaven's treasury

—remember that, Child.

Remember Who I Am and the price I paid, and take care lest your mind reprove what it cannot comprehend.

I AM goodness. I AM compassion. I AM Love.

I AM eternal.

The needs around you are not eternal—the pain of this world will not live forever, for I have overcome the world.[2]

Fierce as death is My Love, relentless as the netherworld

*is My devotion; its flashes are the flashes of fire, its flames
are a blazing fire.[3]*

I AM Love

*And I have been here all the time, loving you, warring
over you, showing you how thin is earth-air.*

*I made human lungs for the richer, heavier winds of
Eden.*

*But it's weightier air than Eden's that I give you now, if
you'll come with courage and draw near.*

*Come, breathe deeply of Me. Draw Kingdom fire from
My lungs,*

*Choose the singing air, rich and heavy with the sound of
My Triune Happiness —*

Come first to enjoy then minister to Me.

And together we'll rejoice as I set my people free.

As the meaning of these words tore through me, something so
clear and clean invaded my heart that I could feel my entire
inner cosmos realigning toward truth. Exhausted from months
spent in the grip of my own private Copernican shift, I watched
like a dazed Galileo as the last of my unruly universe fell back
into place. Planets whizzed past me; stars shot by. Startled into
activity, the moon took up its tidal watch, and my earth shud-
dered on its axis. Slowly, it began to spin away from center
space to cut an outside arc around the sun. Then, and only
then, did I see Him come. God — my dazzling, flamethrowing
God — came streaking over the horizon and a new day, an
everlasting day, dawned in me.

The night was over. My quest had ended and I was left
with order in my heart. I saw, as if for the first time, words I
had read so many times before: "Thou art worthy, O Lord, to
receive glory and honour and power: for thou hast created all

things, and *for thy pleasure they are and were created*" (Revelation 4:11, KJV, italics mine).

Searing a path straight to the core of my being, these words opened wide all the deserted, darkened portions of my heart. Light flooded in, warmth returned, and I responded without restraint to His ancient call:

> "Bring My sons from afar,
>   And My daughters from the ends of the earth,
>   Everyone who is called by My name,
>   And whom I have created for My glory,
>   Whom I have formed, even whom I have
> made. . . .
>   The people whom I have formed for Myself,
>   Will declare My praise." (Isaiah 43:6-7,21)

As if by reflex, my knees bent and my entire being bowed. What privilege, what high purpose, had been entrusted to fragile flesh! He who has His pick of solar symphonies had chosen mankind to sound His praises. This One whose glory is so flawlessly echoed by all the angelic host had turned His ear to hear our whispered worship. It is true, "The heavens declare the glory of God; and the firmament sheweth his handework" (Psalm 19:1, KJV), but His *image* rests on the sons and daughters of Adam.[4]

This then, is our task. It is our unique privilege to offer heaven an everlasting reflection of God's glory, the timeless tale of His amazing goodness to a weary, wrinkled race. From bodies cursed with death, we speak of Life. With the same voices that cry to Him for rescue from pain and grief, we fearlessly declare Him worthy of any earthly loss —*any* personal sacrifice.

This is our reason for living. We are living stones in an eternal temple, priests to a living God.⁵ To this priesthood we bring our greatest passion, our eager energy. Here, on this side of the grave, in full view of Satan and his forces and of God and His angels, we are clothed in our eternal mandate. It is here and now, while the darkness grows stronger and faith is still necessary, that we must embrace our fundamental function: *We were brought into being to engage God's heart, not just to meet man's need.*⁶

That's the purpose of this book: to engage again the heart of God—who alone is worthy of our deepest devotion.. For centuries, the church has gloriously and sacrificially spoken to mankind about God. Now, as the end of the age draws near, we must pursue the heart of God with equal fervor and sacrifice. Yes, we must appeal to Him on behalf of humanity, but we must also seek Him for His own sake. This is what He longs for.⁷ This is the fellowship for which He gave His Son to the earth.

Once embraced, this fellowship with God will produce an earthly witness that no amount of evil can undermine. Out of this passionate exchange will emerge a people who are able to minister effectively to the needs of their neighborhoods because they have first touched the heart of their God. They will face without fear the turmoil of the lives around them because, with arrows drawn directly from *God's* quiver, they will pierce the hearts of men and women with *His* love. Yes, the church will continue to have a witness worthy of the name of Jesus—one that reflects His ministry to His Father, as well as His ministry to humankind.

AFTER MONTHS OF turbulent preparation, the ground had finally been declared ready. I felt the finger of God push this single seed deep into my heart. It took root there in the fall of my twenty-first year and now, years later, I sit in the shade of a maturing truth.

"The chief end of man is to glorify God and enjoy Him forever." With great rejoicing these words have become the theme of my existence. The woven word of God has wrapped me fully round and now I wear these simple sentences everywhere. I never take them off. I sleep in the comfort of their closeness and walk with them through each new day. Never tiring of their pattern, I attend christenings and funerals alike in this single garment; and in this I will be buried, for it is what I want to be wearing when I meet Him face to face. I am sealed for all time in this apparel of praise, cloaked in the sure knowledge that I do not exist for myself or for mankind. I have been created for God.

This is the Bible's claim for every human life. We are created for God. He is the beginning and the end of this sovereign story. *He* is our purpose; He is the "more." Though He may never use the same catechism words with you as He did with me, the ultimate message ends up the same: We are the special object of His love and desire because we have been uniquely shaped by His hand for interaction with His heart. Therefore, our purpose in life is not simply to leave a legacy of good works and kind living. Whatever worthwhile tasks and goals we may pursue here on earth, it is ultimately God's pleasure — not our productivity — that validates our existence.

Neither are we here just to secure our salvation far away from the heat of hell. We have been called to something higher than ensuring an eternity spent in peace instead of pain. As those who have been created for God, the thrust of our existence is not our safety, but God's glory — and His glory is to open to us the truest place of safety and love we will ever know.

Two

TO LOVE THE MUSIC

Whatever our individual ministries may involve, whatever earthly tasks God has given us to do, we carry in our hearts a collective, sacred song—one common to all Christians, sung purely for the pleasure of God.

ARRIVING LATE, I hurried down the halls of the university's music complex. Quick blips of sound hit me from every doorway. Like spinning the tuning dial of an old radio, I heard brief, broken-off snatches of music as I ran past dozens of practice rooms. Coming at last to a small auditorium, I searched for Eric.

Several years had passed since we had last seen each other, but my tall, lanky cousin was unchanged. Gripping his beloved trombone in one hand, he gave me a bony hug and a boyish grin. Memories of the toddler he had once been flooded my mind. I could still see him padding through his home in his pajamas, his unrestrained two-year-old voice singing "Hooo-ya! Hooo-ya!" to his recording of "The Hallelujah Chorus."

Now Eric looked all grown up in his suit and tie— grown up, but still too young to be the guest musician at this master class.

Over the next forty-five minutes, however, as he and his accompanist moved through pieces that grew increasingly difficult, I realized afresh what a masterful musician he is. A trombonist with the Philadelphia Orchestra, Eric was on a brief tour of the Midwestern states and had stopped in Iowa City for this single, two-hour symposium.

As the last notes of a duet from Bach's *Cantata no. 78* died away, Eric turned to the expectant young faces before him. Intense, bright-eyed trombone majors sat scattered throughout the room, eager for advice on joining the world of professional concert musicians.

Loosening the mouthpiece of his trombone, Eric slowly wiped it with a cloth. "How many of you plan to pursue a career with a symphony orchestra?" he asked.

Everywhere in the room, hands went up.

"Okay," he said, glancing around, "of those who raised your hands, how many of you want to play in an orchestra because it seems like a decent way to make a living?"

Expressions turned quizzical and this time only a few students responded.

"How many want to play the trombone professionally because you're good at it?" Eric asked. "It's what you do best and you know that, given the right opportunity, you would succeed?"

Between quick sideways glances around the room, several more students made hesitant responses.

"All right, then," he nodded, "how many of you want to spend your life playing this instrument because you *love* it — you love the trombone and you can't imagine doing anything else. To you this is not just an instrument; it's a way of life. It's as dear to you as a part of your own body and, more than anything else, you want to spend the rest of your life playing it!"

Immediately the mood in the room shifted; enthusiasm surged. No one was hesitant now. Of course! This was the test of a true musician—love of one's instrument. This surely was the ultimate measure of motives. Everywhere, arms shot into the air.

Eric paused. "That's good," he said, looking slowly from face to face, ". . . but it's not enough."

Startled, the students grew still. Like the gradual descent of a hundred helium balloons, limp arms sank slowly, silently, onto the seats.

"It's not enough to love your instrument," Eric repeated. "Loving the trombone is not enough to sustain you through the decades of stress and monotony of a symphonic career. If that's all you have, you won't make it—you'll burn out."

Turning to put his trombone in its case, Eric continued quietly but clearly: "To stay emotionally alive in a professional symphony orchestra, you have to love what the composer has written. You have to love the *music!*"

THIS BOOK IS about learning to love The Music. It is about learning to reach past the pull of our own ministries, past the love we may have for our own instruments, to engage the heart of God. It is about learning to stay positioned before the Father the same way Jesus did—responding to Him first and to everything else second.

What is The Music? What is the song that every born-again believer has been called to learn and to love? It is the song of fiery devotion between the members of the Godhead. It is the music of their eternal, unsunderable oneness. It is the sound of their triumphant war cry, the ancient echo of their triune victory song. In this song—in this ageless anthem— resides all the sacred awareness of the Godhead: the perichoresis of God.[1]

Loving The Music means entering into the very life and fellowship of the Godhead. It means knowing, through the power of the Holy Spirit, the same freedom, the same extraordinary *fun* that Jesus has with His Father. It means knowing the same unrestrained joy of communion that He has with the Spirit, and it means joining the revelry of the Godhead as they bring to completion the plan of redemption set in motion by their love so many ages ago.

HOW DO WE enter the life and fellowship of the Godhead? The journey dealing with that question begins in the next chapter. At this point, however, I can tell you something of what will happen as we take this journey together and participate more and more fully in the grand, passionate exchange of our God's "inner life."

We will find that the very things that move the heart of God begin to move our hearts as well. No longer will we be preoccupied by our own thoughts, but by His. We will not be mesmerized by the sound of our voices speaking our words, but by His voice speaking His Word. Ultimately, as we partake not only of God's tenderness and patience but also of His strength and fire, we will begin to express the very life of Jesus Christ. We will hear The Music of the Godhead more and more clearly, and hearing, we will participate in the passionate exchange.

How do I know this will happen? Because Jesus promised it. It was His prayer before His death and His provision upon rising again:

> "Neither for these alone do I pray [it is not for their
> sake only that I make this request], but also for all
> those who will ever come to believe in . . . Me
> through their word and teaching, that they all may
> be one, [just] as You, Father, are in Me and I in

You, that they also may be one in Us, so that the
world may believe and be convinced that You sent
Me." (John 17:20-21, AMP)

Any gospel short of this truth is not the gospel of Jesus Christ.
He gave us nothing less than adoption ("you have received a
spirit of adoption as sons by which we cry out, 'Abba!
Father!'"[2]), which entitles us to the complete legal, social, and
emotional life—the life of love—that is His home. "If anyone
loves Me," Jesus said, "he will keep My word; and My Father
will love him, and We will come to him, and make Our abode
with him" (John 14:23).

We are joint heirs with Jesus, not just someday in heaven,
but now, on this earth. The apostle Paul wrote, "The Spirit
Himself bears witness with our spirit that we are children of
God, and if children, heirs also, heirs of God and fellow heirs
with Christ" (Romans 8:16-17). The word for the kind of life
God has given to Christians is *zoe*, meaning "the absolute fullness of life, both essential and ethical, which belongs to God."[3]

SO, WE HAVE been made sons and heirs—participants with
Jesus in the fullness of His life. There is nothing He has with-
held. His very nature has been given to us.[4]

Are we, then, in some way "equal" to God? No. We are the
creatures; He is the Creator. He is to be worshiped; we are the
worshipers. We are dependent for every breath; He is all-suffi-
cient, self-sustaining—He *is* our breath. We come to God not
as equals, but as those who serve Him.

We have, however, held back the fullness of our service. We
have served God by ministering to those in need around us, but
we have felt unprepared—uncertain—how to minister to
Him directly. Though sensing we were made for more—

indeed, made for God Himself—we have not known what that requires of us. How do we "minister" to a God who needs nothing? How do we touch a God we cannot see? Understanding how to minister *to* God from the confines of this earth without doing something *for* Him has been difficult to understand.

Most of us want a deeper interaction with God. We truly desire a more vital, spontaneous exchange of hearts. We know we will live in God's presence in heaven, but we struggle to know how to live in His presence here on earth. Though convinced that we will enjoy great intimacy with Him throughout eternity, we don't know how to experience such closeness here and now, especially amid the crush of daily deadlines and demands.

So we wait it out. We fix our hope on the next life and expect that a magical, effortless intimacy with God will develop the moment we leave this world behind. Emotionally, we withdraw from the daunting notion of ministering to a God we can't see, and turn our attention instead to the demands of human need. We do this not because it is our first and truest calling, but because the needs are obvious, tangible, and urgent. We can *do* something in response. We turn our hearts toward relationships in which the interactions are "real" and forthcoming, and the results are quantifiable.

The only problem is that this does not satisfy the deepest desire of God's heart; it does not secure His full pleasure because it does not account for the full mandate that is on our lives. We were created for fellowship and ministry to God,[5] not just to the world around us.

All Christians are, by definition, ministers to God first— then to people. The Scriptures tell us that the first and greatest commandment is to "love the Lord your God with all your heart, and with all your soul, and with all your mind, and with all your strength" (Mark 12:30). The second is to "love your neighbor as yourself" (Mark 12:31).

Our ministry to God is eternal in nature and requires the ongoing gift of our hearts for the sole purpose of His pleasure. Our ministry to humankind, though important in its own right, must always be the result of our communion with God, never the other way around. Any work that we do among men, women, and children here on earth must emerge directly from our intimacy with God. Nothing less can sustain it.[6] Any comfort we give, any help we offer, must always be authorized and empowered by our contact with God's heart. Everything we do to fulfill the second commandment must always pass through the filter of the first.

If this is true, what about all the other things God has asked us to do? What about the good works the Bible says must accompany our faith?[7] Shouldn't we be servants to those around us? Doesn't the Bible say to feed the hungry, clothe the naked, visit the prisoner — in short, to lay down our lives that the gospel can go forth and the life of Christ can be seen in the earth?

Yes! Clearly. Absolutely. *But we must never give to men what belongs only to God.*[8]

What belongs to God is our gaze — the open shutter of our soul stretching wide in the light of His quest for communion. What belongs to God is the person He formed in our mother's womb, the person we were before the voices of this world began to tell us who we are. That person, that virginal listening life, belongs to God alone, and we dare not give it to another. We dare not shift our focus or redefine our purpose to accommodate something less than the death of Jesus deserves. After all, would He have died simply to generate an army of do-gooders — a team of nice people who mean well but who can't accomplish in a lifetime what angels can do in a moment? If efficiency and productivity were the true issues, would He really have picked *us?*

No. Something bigger is going on. Jesus died to restore to His Father the unashamed gaze of Eden's lost children. He died to recapture for His Father the "orchestra" of voices that were created for more—more than the love of their own instruments, more than the love of their own ministries. He came to baptize us with the same communion, the same passionate exchange of fellowship that has always marked the inner life of the Godhead.[9]

Because this is true—because we were brought into His kingdom to participate in His life—God does not allow us to stay safely nestled in a pocket of earthly productivity untouched by intimacy with Him. He pursues us.

MY HUSBAND AND I knew a pastor who, as a child, used to dream of the day he would go into the ministry and have a church of his own. So real was his dream that, as a teenager driving the tractor on his family's farm, he spent hours preaching to the open fields and planning for the day he would serve God by serving people.

Finally, after completing his education, he and his wife began a fledgling congregation. Soon larger and larger crowds were gathering each Sunday morning. The fulfillment of his lifelong ambition seemed on the verge of realization, when suddenly everything came to a crashing halt.

Through a series of circumstances and personal prodding, God asked this man to give up his pastorate. During times of prayer, he clearly heard the Lord ask him to relinquish all of his work. The exact words God spoke to his heart were, "Would you be willing for Me to put to death your ministry?"

Days and nights of agonized struggle followed. "Lord!" he cried incredulously. "All I've ever wanted to do is be a minister to your people! Everything I've trained for is just beginning to happen. People are getting saved; the church is thriving; I'm preaching well; and hurting people are being helped. I'm doing all this for *You!* How can You want me to step down now?"

As unbelievable as it seemed, the crushing conviction of God's will grew inside him until he faced the inevitable question: "Is it the ministry that I love or is it God that I love?"

Until now the two had seemed inseparable. To love God had always meant to serve people. It had always been a foregone conclusion that one begat the other. Now everything was a tangle of mixed motives and fading dreams. Like an unbroken colt, his heart bucked and reared as it realized the nature of the bridle and bit it was being asked to wear. Heaviness and grief settled on him. All the fondly held promises for his future were being recalled—God was demanding the life of his Isaac.

So he relinquished his pastorate—as an act of worship. "Lord," he said, "I don't understand this; I don't know why You're requiring it of me, but I love You more than I love my ministry, so here it is. I give it back to you. If the only thing I'm ever allowed to do in Your kingdom is worship You, it will be enough. If no one ever hears me preach but You, it will be enough. My ministry to You is more important than my ministry to people."

That day, a true "minister of the gospel" was born—someone who ministers to God first and to people second. A year later, God restored this man to the pastorate and blessed him there for more than a quarter of a century.

With or without his pastorate, this man knew he would never be the same. Any weekday morning, before facing the needs of his people, he could be found on his knees in the church prayer room ministering to the heart of his God.

～

BECAUSE WE WILL minister to God someday in heaven, we can start here on earth. If we have been called to share the dwelling place of the Most High God, we begin now. If eternity is ours . . . *so is the present!*

Now is the time to approach God with courage; now is the time to enter His nearness—here, in this life, without waiting for death to "free" us. If Jesus is our Savior and Lord, we have already died with Him and are already free.[10] We are, in fact, by God's own proclamation, a "royal priesthood, a holy nation" (1 Peter 2:9), equipped and set apart for Him alone. We minister to the heart of God here and now, not just in the age to come!

Every born-again Christian belongs to this "new priesthood" by virtue of the death and resurrection of Jesus Christ. The book of Hebrews makes it clear that the death of Jesus not only fulfilled the old law, it also inaugurated a new one. Not only did it complete the old covenant, it also set in motion the new covenant; and with the new covenant came the new priesthood—blood offspring of Jesus, the great and final High Priest.[11]

As such, this priesthood into which we have been born is *ministerial,* not substitutionary, in nature. We do not offer atoning sacrifices, perform ritual cleansings, or intercede for each other based upon personal merit. The priesthood of which we are members doesn't in any way mediate the new covenant. The Bible tells us clearly that "there is one God, and one mediator also between God and men, the man Christ Jesus" (1 Timothy 2:5).

Instead, we minister. We minister to the people of this earth humbly, graciously, and enthusiastically, but it is to God alone that the ultimate ministrations and allegiance of this royal priesthood belong. We are equipped and set apart for Him here and now, not just in the age to come!

In part 2 of this book, we will see that God Himself helps us choose more than just servanthood, and that it is His hand that brings us into the fullness of fellowship — into the celebration of His own heart as He recaptures the trusting, focused gaze of His children.

In part 3 we will discover that ministering to God is a unique expression of our walk with God: It is worship, but more than worship; it is prayer, but more than prayer. We will talk about what it means to minister to God in our everyday lives amid demanding schedules and pressing deadlines, all in the course of doing with integrity the earthly work God has given us to do. In this way, we will discover practical steps that each of us can take to develop a personal ministry to Him.

Before that, however, we will look at the nature of the fellowship we have been called to enter. In the pages just ahead, we will talk about intimacy with God — why we often find it so intimidating, and how we should respond in the face of our fear.

Three

THE FURNACE OF
FELLOWSHIP

Jesus is our example in all things pertaining to God. His interaction with His Father is our truest model of ministry to God. To become effective in ministry to God's heart, therefore, we must become like Jesus. This we do, not simply by approximating and reproducing the actions of Jesus toward His Father, but by partaking of the very life that He has with His Father.

*I*F I SHUT my eyes and think back, I can remember the rare and wonderful campfires of my childhood. I remember the feel of a cool, clear autumn evening, the smell of September smoke, and the general hubbub of activity as our family dragged lawn chairs into position around a stack of dry, ready logs.

Our preparations were always rustic and simple. The remains of our picnic supper were stashed in the cooler and sticky fingers were rinsed at the pump, then we kids headed off for one final romp through the Illinois woods, looking for bits of dry bark and tinder.

Finally, after Dad coaxed a small flicker into full flame, we'd settle ourselves for the evening ahead. Faces hot, backs cold, we stared for hours into the brightness of the blaze. Huddled safely within the warm ring of the night fire, we felt protected from the darkness, shut in with the sweet, heavy scent of a dying summer.

Endless cycles of conversation passed between us with no one feeling the need to see faces, check expressions, or meet each other's eyes. None of us seemed to notice each other's movements at all. We were watching the fire. Only the fire seemed to move. Only the random gestures of the flame's fingers held our attention, and we sat thoroughly entertained by their every darting movement, mesmerized by every shift of glowing coals.

Together we watched and waited expectantly. As time passed and the flames descended slowly, deeply into the logs, a small, throbbing structure would appear. As the wood was carved and hollowed out by the heat, an inner chamber of liquid fire formed. What was once a pile of dry timber had become a searing, throbbing sanctuary of light. Something in there was alive—we could all sense it. The white-hot center of the fire was surging, pounding—we could see its pulse!

Sticks were sent in to explore. As the conversation circled around and around, we jabbed and poked among the inner embers of the fire. Probing the places of intense heat, we tried, with our long wooden fingers, to feel the pulsating heart before us. We traced the great glowing arteries, touching, testing, searching for the source of life within.

Finally, with our eyes dry from the heat, our bodies stiff, and our stories told, we prepared to leave. The sticks were pulled from the fire, their ends red and glowing and alive.

~

WE'VE SEEN JESUS as the cozy, approachable flame that welcomes us. We have settled ourselves near His gentle warmth and, like squatters gathered around a campfire, we've watched His every movement with keen interest.

Sitting near Him in the light of His love, we have found our peace. Here we have talked freely, shared openly, and explored the inner working of His ways. We have felt at ease as we probed the mysterious pathways of His power and pondered the endless nuances of His words. Feeling protected and safe, we have sent our "sticks" into His presence and rested securely in the knowledge that they will return to us bright with borrowed fire. We have grown well content with the diffused light of our Lord and the steady comfort His presence provides.

But we forget. We lose track of who He is and where He comes from. We think we are safe, but we are not.

Jesus comes from the flaming furnace of a raging, intimate fellowship, and there is nothing entirely "safe" here. There never has been. Jesus is the very substance of a love so full and fiery that even heaven must work to withstand the force of it. Even the angels fail to find a leisurely, relaxed position with which to greet the exposed glory of the triune God.[1]

So it is that, on occasion, our gentle Jesus chooses to surprise us. Sometimes when we least expect it (perhaps we're positioned for a time of warm, chatty prayer or drowsy, uneventful worship), He rips past the protective space between us and, like a night fire gone awry, sears us with eternity. He comes close, really close, and we feel the scorching heat of a presence too bright, too beautiful to be endured quietly.

Pulling back, we search for the more predictable Jesus that we trust — the Jesus who warms but never burns, whose light comforts but never blinds. We search for the Jesus of our past experience, the "perfect gentleman" who patiently encouraged our troubled heart, unscrambled our tangled thoughts, and beckoned rather than pushed us past the points of our resistance.

We search, but He is gone; in His place is something not entirely gentlemanly or mindful of our boundaries. Having unwittingly lost track of our quiet campfire, we face a forest fire instead. In place of our cozy puddle of warmth, there before us is a massive, roaring tower of flame! All our warning systems go into effect; all our alarms start to scream, and instantly we know we are in danger. Suddenly, we are facing the grand, unfathomable passion of God—the glorious inferno of intimacy that is the Godhead—Christ's home.

Somehow, without anyone tipping us off, we know that this overpowering presence would not yield to idle exploration. Instinctively, we sense that no poking, probing stick would come back to us glowing. It would not come back at all, and we stand shaken before the force of such a fellowship.

THE SCRIPTURES TELL us God is living, eternal, and mysterious in all His ways. He is uncreated, self-existent, with no beginning and no end. He is simultaneously Three and One. Each Person, each expression of the Godhead, carries within Himself the full attributes of God. Each one is God; One God . . . not three. The Father, Son, and Holy Spirit have been together always. Never have they not been one and the same God.[2]

Nothing from outside God in any way holds Him together. Nothing binds Him to Himself but Himself. There are no forces at work to confine or restrain Him, for He transcends all the natural laws that affect us. He exists far beyond all boundaries that give shape and form to our lives. Everything that is constraining to God is done from within.

"Within" there is a covenant of communion, a fellowship of profound and passionate faithfulness. There is nothing passive here. This is a fiery blast furnace of intimacy and love. Only to the demands of their own internal covenant, only to the force of their own sovereign celebration, do the members of the Godhead submit, and nothing external is allowed to violate their union. They are ever One, never separately three.

A fierce fidelity stands guard over this churning crossfire of mutual love and devotion. Absolute allegiance shoots like liquid fire throughout the Godhead. Nothing so interests the Son as the glory of the Father. Nothing is more important to the Father than the love of His Son, and nothing so satisfies the Spirit as the glorious communion between them. A piercing, searing symmetry of honor and adoration penetrates the heart of each member in an eternal fusion of fellowship.

So ferocious is this fellowship, so fluid is this fiery exchange, so *terrifying* is the beauty of this interaction, that no mortal can see it and live. No one uninvited can approach the vortex of this virtue and survive. No one unshielded can safely witness the blinding dimensions of this devotion, for nothing in heaven or on the earth is allowed to interfere with this intimacy; nothing carrying the scent of "strange fire" is tolerated in the midst of this white-hot holiness.[3]

So compelling is the power of this union that God need only speak His own name, "I AM," and all of time is swallowed by eternity. We are time-bound. We are born, we age, and we die. He who transcends all time and space simply "is." He is eternally the same; He is One. "Hear, O Israel! The LORD is our God, the LORD is one!" (Deuteronomy 6:4).

It is out of this intimate union that the Spirit of Jesus, the Holy Spirit, comes to the earth. He comes not just as a spark thrown from the eternal furnace. He is not resident with us as a splintered-off subsection of God, disengaged and sent down to represent God. He *is* God. The very fullness of the Godhead dwells in Him, and when we open ourselves to the love of Jesus, it is *we* who are probed and poked. It is *our* hearts that are searched and explored. We are cleansed and made ready for the consuming fire that cannot be kept a safe stick's-distance away. We are prepared for the One whose love must ultimately brand us deep within.

THROUGHOUT THE DAYS of Israel's patriarchs, priests, and kings, God often represented Himself to the earth in the form of fire. He came as a flaming torch to Abram, a fiery bush to Moses, and a pillar of flame to the nation of Israel as they fled Egypt. Many times, He fell as a consuming fire of judgment upon the enemies of Israel and received with consecrating fire the sacrifices of David, Solomon, and Elijah.

The last recorded manifestation of God's fire on earth took place shortly after Jesus' return to His Father. Tongues of fire appeared on the heads of the disciples on a Jewish feast day known as Pentecost.[4] This is the day the Holy Spirit came publicly and with power to take up residence within humankind. That being the case, it seems that God should have sent doves to rest on the heads of each of the disciples to symbolize their infilling. He did not. He sent fire.

I believe God was determined that the earth should see not only that the Spirit had come, but also that the Spirit brought with Him the same surging celebration that was present at Creation, the same fiery exchange of passion that has marked the inner life of the Godhead throughout the ages. Carrying the flaming insignia of an eternal, unquenchable love, the Holy Spirit brought the towering holiness of Yahweh as well as the penetrating presence of Jesus — to live within us.

The Spirit came as fire and as a mighty, rushing wind, ushering in the age of our adoption — the age of God as "our"

Father.[5] Through the death and resurrection of His Son Jesus, all who believed were now made sons and daughters, partakers of the flame, joint heirs of the fire of His fellowship.

There in Jerusalem, in the shadow of the temple, a greater temple was formed—one made of human hearts.[6] There, in the shadow of the Law, a greater law was given—the law of everlasting love.[7] God would no longer meet with mankind only amid the smoke and stone of ritual sacrifice. No longer would His favor fall merely on the keeping of feasts and the shearing of foreskins. All things had finally been claimed within the Godhead; all citizens were now subject to a higher court than Caesar; all authority was now held by One with nail prints in His hands.

The tongues of fire were God's divine declaration of intent. They were the searing seal of His new covenant. From this day forward, the God of Israel would inhabit every circumcised heart and dwell forever with any who lived within the New Law of His love. He would now tabernacle in the redeemed hearts of men and women throughout the earth and commune with any who worshiped Him in spirit and in truth.[8] He would, from this time on, make the temples of their bodies His new meeting place and fall again with holy fire upon each *living* sacrifice.[9]

Four

THE FEAR OF FELLOWSHIP

Though most of us have sensed the greater call of God on our lives, we are often afraid of moving forward into a more intimate fellowship with Him. Even though there are countless scriptural assurances of our welcome, we struggle with fear of the very thing we were created for.

MANY OF US who make up the church, the body of Christ on earth, have scratched out an existence for ourselves between two fears: the isolation of hell and the intimacy of heaven. Wedged between these opposing realities, we have formed a third world, not in the grave but not in God's glory, not back in Egypt but not in Canaan either. For years we have peered from the shadows, but still stand shy of life—not in hell, not in heaven. All in all, it is a strangely protective purgatory we have found for ourselves—a dubious sort of safety that endeavors to shield us from the grip of the Enemy *and* the presence of God.

I know a much-loved little boy who, when he was three, would pray in tiny, simple, fresh words to a God he was just beginning to know. By the age of five, however, he was praying tight, choppy prayers always using the same words: "Dear God, thank you for this good day and this good night. Please take care of Daddy and Mommy. Please don't let any robbers come tonight. Please don't let the house catch on fire. Please help me not to have bad dreams. Amen."

This fairly direct set of requests could take up to five minutes if, for some reason, he faltered over the exact wording or forgot one of the crucial elements. His little face would scrunch up, his tiny fingers pressed hard into a proper, sweaty prayer-fist, and he would struggle to get everything said so that nothing bad would happen.

As his parents, it hurt us to watch this scene. My husband and I wrestled with our desire to break into "the system" and put him in touch with the real God, the living God, so that he could pray real, living prayers. Even so, we knew that only God could truly reveal Himself to the heart of a five-year-old.

Somehow, in two brief years of our son consciously interacting with God, ritual had already emerged. Where had it come from? At what point did the formula become safe and the real God fade behind a veil of fear? When did the past take over the present? This prayer was the true expression of his little heart the first time he prayed it, maybe even the first few times. But now it had become a well-worn lucky charm, an incantation.

Even more difficult for us to see was the peace that would settle in as soon as the ritual was successfully completed. The fidgeting would stop; his face would relax; his duty was done. It's not that he didn't believe in God. He most fervently did. That's why it was so important to get it right. He felt that the things of God, those things that already had meaning, had to be offered again and again.

MANY OF US hide a frightened five-year-old deep inside our adulthood. We feel compelled to return to that time when we sensed a genuine communication with God, then try to repeat it verbatim. That time when we really felt His presence becomes a prototype for all future interaction, and we're confident of His pleasure only if we repeat the performances of our past. Ritual, often the second- and third-generation hardening of an experience that was once full of life, can become our refuge from current communion with God.

It takes courage to live in the present with a fiery God of intimacy and adventure, especially when His primary agenda is to form the full expression of His Son in us. We try to stay pliable in His hand but fear what He may ultimately require of us. We see the necessity and inevitability of change but feel secure only if we get to regulate the amount of pressure we're under in the process. Even though we have every intention of cooperating with God as He moves us toward maturity, we end up protecting ourselves instead.

IT HAS NOT always been this way. As individuals we haven't always been so tentative in our approach to God. We can remember that even though our first steps toward Jesus required great faith, we responded well. We trusted Him. We came simply, unfalteringly, into the stream that drew us to God, and there we willingly died to our sin. In this baptism of our souls, we died to our old nature and we received a new one.

Gradually, however, as our faces broke the surface of the stream, as we shook the water from our eyes and gazed ahead, we recognized with some shock the requirements of our new life. Startled, we surveyed the fullness of the fellowship that waited on the far shore.

We had believed, accepted, and acted upon this truth: to live with God, we must die to ourselves.[1] We knew that to be born again we had to embrace not only the cradle but also the cross; the Bible says so. This, however, is only half the story.

The Scriptures also tell us that if we follow Jesus into death, we must follow Him into His resurrection life as well.[2] *If* we die, then we *must* live again. God requires it.[3] In fact, because He requires new life, He also provides for it. In the Father's plan, resurrection always follows the faith that the cross entails.

So, if we wade into the stream, we must wade back out on the other side. It is not enough to tread water at the spot of our salvation, caught in the crosscurrent of the past and the future. We are not meant to swim endless circles around the site of our surrender, remembering only the glory of that moment. We are called to cross over into fellowship with God, into the ongoing glory of His presence.

We have been called and we want to respond, but it is here that fear often wells up within us. It seems a dangerous resurrection that we face. We are still flesh and blood and, as desperately as we want to be with God, we instinctively protect ourselves from the white-hot intimacy that is now our new home. Our arms go up, not in surrender but as a shield, not in welcome but in withdrawal.

Even though this is what Christ died to give us, even though this blinding Light is the other side of our salvation, we cover our eyes and our expectations. We back away.

Like hunted animals scratching at a wall, we search for the crack between death and resurrection, hoping for entrance into a sliver of safety—a crevice of cooler, softer light. With fear as our guide, we scramble for a protected place somewhere between the silence of the tomb and the sound of God's voice.

The intensity of God's devotion is more than we bargained for. The ultimate tone of His intentions is unnerving. We feel pushed from behind to embrace things we don't understand.

We knew that Jesus would be our friend, our companion, our eternal habitation, but we didn't expect to be *His*. We knew God called us to minister to those around us; we just didn't know He'd called us to Him first. We understood that Christ carried the weight of our sin in His mortal body, but never counted on carrying the weight of His glory in ours!

We wanted a discreet, civilized agreement with God, not the crucible of a covenant. We wanted to be with Him in heaven someday; now He's rushing heaven into our hearts — to dwell in us. We wanted to have friendly fellowship, but certainly not fusion, nothing as confining as "oneness"! We wanted to minister *for* Him, not *to* Him. We wanted a method, not a marriage.

But again, the Scriptures are clear. It is marriage that we're headed for.[4] Corporately, we are the bride of Christ, not His maid. There will be no stiff, staid communion between us. There will be no mild, isolated servanthood. A vow has been made, His word has been given, and we have given ours.

IT IS HERE that we recognize one of Christianity's overarching truths: God has never given us a choice about the *nature* of what we have been called to enter. The only choice we have is whether or not to go in. Our God is truly a "consuming fire" (Hebrews 12:29), and this fire will not be curtailed simply for our comfort. His blinding, blazing light was evident long before the age began, and it will not be darkened or diffused merely to save our sight. Our God will not be less than who He is.

So we have a choice. We can enter the place of His dwelling, or we can stand clear. We can proceed in faith or we can falter; but we must know this: there is no heaven but this one. There is no safe, mist-covered neutrality awaiting us on the other side. There is no removed, private accommodation somewhere in our future, for the fire of intimacy is the very nature of the Father's house. God's heaven is where He is and there is no buffer zone between. There is no way for us to stand on the outside of intimacy and still know salvation. We either face the fire of fellowship with Him or the fire of isolation and hell without Him.[5]

This call to oneness and intimacy is binding for every believer. For us, it is the only choice. Never has walking in the fire of God's presence been an optional activity for those who genuinely want to follow Jesus. Never has the pursuit of God's manifest glory been reserved only for those who want the "advanced course" in Christianity. It is all He has offered to any of us. There is no easier way. There is no middle ground for us—for there is no life in limbo, no resurrection power in the netherworld of neutrality.

It is not enough to die to sin; we must live to Christ. It is not enough to wake from the sleep of the grave; we must step forth and shed all the trappings of death. We must strip ourselves of soiled grave clothes. Throwing off guilt, we embrace grace; throwing off comfort, we pursue Christ. He deserves our first loyalty, our first allegiance. His heart is our first ministry, and the demands of our other ministries must wait!

If it is truly God we desire, then it is the furnace of fellowship we must enter. If it is the name of Christ we wear, then He is the One we must follow. As *Christ*-ians, we go where Jesus Christ goes—deep into the dwelling place of the Father.

Five

PARTAKERS OF THE FLAME

*What, then, can be said? Must we enter God's pres-
ence, this frightening arena of intimacy and oneness? Yes, we must. Is it really necessary that we go
there, that we pursue this "dangerous" destination?
Yes, it is. For our God has called us by name . . .
into His life . . . into His glory. He loves us and
wants us with Him where He is.[1]*

WE CANNOT GENUINELY know Jesus without the brand
of that knowledge marking our hearts forever. As His
influence becomes more and more active within us, we begin
to resonate with the same fluid, fiery exchange that accompa-
nies every interaction of the Godhead.

It is into the ever-deepening dimensions of this intimacy
that God calls us. It is an ever-clearer image of this oneness —
this Music — He commissions us to carry. Caught in the
whirling centrifuge of loving conversation between the
Father and the Son, we have become communicators with
the living God. Under the influence of the Holy Spirit, we
have become participants in the great exchange of hearts
that spans all time and space. Hearing the cry of God's
heart and responding with the cry of our own, we enter the
lightning-like volley of the Godhead's own passionate
exchange.

We enter this exchange not as equals with God but as ministers to Him. We participate as those who have had this place prepared for them by the blood of Jesus Christ. We come before the face of this intimacy knowing full well that, except for the protection of Christ's righteousness, we would be instantly destroyed.[2]

Covered in Christ, however, we are not destroyed. Instead, we live! Actually, we live "abundantly beyond all that we ask or think" (Ephesians 3:20), for we have been seated "with [Christ] in the heavenly places" (Ephesians 2:6). Clothed in the virtue of Jesus Christ, we are escorted into the very arena of God's own Oneness.[3]

We are not kept at a distance. We are not removed to a more respectful, remote location. There is no separate, roped-off corner of the cosmos from which we are to merely watch in wonder and observe in amazement. We have been called *in!*

The gospel of John reflects nothing forced or grudging in Christ's manner as He cried out, "Father, I desire that they also, whom Thou hast given Me, be with Me where I am, in order that they may behold My glory" (17:24).

We have been called in "to behold" Christ's glory. The Greek word used here for "behold" is *theoreo* and, as used in this passage, it means to "experience in the sense of partaking."[4] We partake of Christ's life and His glory. As with all followers of Jesus throughout the ages, we are called into the same exchange of fire that Christ has always known!

So, what does this "exchange of fire" look like on this side of heaven? In part 3 I will show you a glimpse of what it has looked like for me. Before that, however, I want to tell you something of how it has *felt*. Given all the allusions to fire, it probably seems wise to prepare for a meteor shower. Actually, interacting with God in the furnace of His fellowship has, for me, felt very much the opposite. Things have been much less intimidating than I expected. Perhaps the closest I can come to it scripturally is a spiritualized version of Shadrach, Meshach, and Abednego's fiery furnace—lots of walking around, talking with Jesus.

For all the overwhelming truth of the fellowship we are called to enter, Jesus makes it very approachable, very much our home too. Knowing I am "dust" and that I "see through a glass darkly," He has worked with me in ways that make sense to my everyday life. I have truly felt Him to be with me as I enter the presence of the Father. True to His name, He has been my Immanuel (God with us), as I have drawn near. The Holy Spirit has counseled me with Scripture as I have battled with feelings of unworthiness, presumption, and fear. I am consistently encouraged to move forward, for "He is able to save forever those who draw near to God through Him, since He always lives to make intercession for them" (Hebrews 7:25), and "Since therefore, brethren, we have confidence to enter the holy place by the blood of Jesus, by a new and living way which He inaugurated for us through the veil, that is, His flesh, and since we have a great priest [Jesus] over the house of God, let us draw near in full assurance of faith." (Hebrews 10:19-22).

Over the years I have realized that my behavior in the furnace of fellowship depends upon my trust in what Jesus accomplished on the cross. If I am relaxed and at peace, confident of my welcome and ready to step forward into fellowship (without trying to win my way in through good behavior), it is only because I am trusting in the integrity of God's Word to me. I am scripturally on solid ground. If I am fearful and self-conscious, aware primarily of myself, my shortcomings, and my sin, I know that I am relying on my righteousness, not the righteousness of Jesus. To this very point Hebrews 10:38

speaks when it says, "But My righteous one shall live by faith; and if he shrinks back, My soul has no pleasure in him."

Though I have been shown my sinful heart many times in that place of fellowship, I have never been alone at the time. Jesus has always stood with me, helping me to hear the truth about myself. I have never been asked to bear the burden of my own sin. In fact, in the furnace of fellowship, I have found the opposite. If there's a struggle over sin, it's because I feel that I should do something to help out, some kind of penance—to make me trustable again. I have been challenged again and again to honor the enormity of what Jesus has done by not trying to supplement it. Just the notion that I have something with which to complete the sacrifice of Jesus is as nonsensical as offering a saltshaker to the sea. In the arena of righteousness I *must* trust—anything else is foolishness and presumption. The fact that I am actually alive and well in the interior of this communion is proof enough of the adequacy of Christ's sacrifice on my behalf.

So, as I learn to take the place that has been prepared for me, as I participate in the great, passionate exchange, I find that because of Jesus I have been given everything I need to satisfy God and to sustain a ministry to Him that will have a profound and loving impact upon His heart.

WE KNOW THE Bible assures us of our welcome in God's presence. What then, does it tell us about the defining characteristics of this God who has welcomed us? What should we expect to find as we approach Him? As we turn again to the Scriptures, we find that its pages do more than describe God's actions—they reveal *who* He is. Statements that come to us in the declarative "God is" format clarify those characteristics that make up the essence of the God we serve. As we seek to minister to Him, three such statements become essential to our understanding:

1. "Holy is the Lord God" (Revelation 4:8).
2. "God is love" (1 John 4:16).
3. "Our God is a consuming fire" (Hebrews 12:29).

These three statements are important because they tell us what to expect when we come before the living God. The first one tells us that our God is holy. Because He is holy, our ministry to Him must be the same; it must function through the righteousness of Jesus Christ alone. As I expressed above, it can have no presumptive self-reliance, for we must remain completely dependent upon Him—even as we seek to minister to Him. Our ministry can have no sinful, self-serving aspect, for its goal is to maintain a genuine focus upon God. The life of Jesus in us makes it possible for our ministry to God to be holy, even as He is holy.

Second, we recognize that the nature of God is love. He is guided by His affections and thoroughly resolved to pursue relationship with us. The relationship He desires is one of love, not of mutual need. The Scriptures indicate that God seeks us because He *loves* us, not because He needs us. John 3:16 does not say, "For God so needed the world, that He sent His only begotten Son." Neither does it say, "For the world so needed God, that He sent His only Son." Instead it says, "For God so *loved* the world, that He gave His only begotten Son, that whoever believes in Him should not perish, but have eternal life" (italics mine).

God's motivation for interaction with mankind has *always* been love, not need. This statement may appear heretical; it can sound as if our need is unimportant and therefore gets passed over. Not at all. The very opposite is at work. Love is stronger than need (indeed it is stronger than death).[5] Love encompasses our need and not only meets it but also dismantles it. It is the most powerful force for freedom that exists, "for the greatest of these is love."[6]

When we approach God in ministry, then, we align ourselves with the love-standard He has set. We do this by receiving His love for us and, in an act of genuine reciprocation, respond out of our love for Him.

One of the essential aspects of a loving interaction between two persons is its genuineness, its honesty. If the love we have for God is real, we come to Him as we really are (determined not to hide from Him) and allow Him to speak truth to us. Whatever means of Bible study or Scripture reading we use, this posture of vulnerability is essential. We come to Him confident of His love but also conscious of our need to be changed. We invite God to do this work of change in us by focusing on His nature, not our own. We respond to *Him,* not to our own failings. By dwelling in Him, by filling the scope of our vision with His image, we will grow in love for Him and, as Jesus taught in John 14:23, if we truly love Him we will keep His Word. Our behavior will be in response to the focus of our affection.

Third, we recognize that our God is a consuming fire. This means that everything He touches is in some way branded by His passionate nature. This is true whether He "touches" with judgment or tender communion. His fire is part and parcel of all that He is—the flaming hallmark of all that He does. He is never passive or apathetic. His holiness is not a static, doctrinal theory, but an unrelenting, searing truth. His love, though often the warm, glowing embrace with which He soothes our pain, can also become the arresting, fiery embrace with which He cleans and cauterizes the deepest of our wounds. This is a good thing. This is an aspect of God's nature I greatly admire and appreciate. Though He knows we are fragile and easily singed, He is committed to our purity. Because He knows that He *is worthy* of our purity, He pursues it in spite of the pain it may cause.

So God is not a nodding, docile patriarch. He is not mildly entertained by our escapades or coolly disinterested in the world He created. He is profoundly passionate about everything that has secured His devotion. If, therefore, we want to minister effectively to this passionate God, we invite Him to be who He really is with us. We don't try to tame Him and make Him "safer" to be around. We ask Him to make us bolder, stronger in His presence.

By the same token, we don't try to tame ourselves. We don't let our heads take what is true for our hearts and domesticate it until it's acceptable to our more sedate, cerebral side. As Westerners long in the grip of a cold, mechanistic mindset, this can take some practice. Showing our emotions—being passionate—seems to happen more naturally for us in a traffic jam than in a prayer meeting.

So, when talking to God and ministering to Him, we take pains *not* to squeeze into poised politeness all that our hearts want to say. We allow the full measure of our own passion to express itself as we respond to Him; we pursue Him boldly, intentionally. Long after our needs have been met, we come, extending to Him the unrestrained reach of our hearts—stretching toward His.

AS THOSE WHO carry within our hearts the very nature of Jesus Christ, we can come to God just as Jesus did. This truth unlocks all that is ours as we learn to love The Music. Our willingness to believe we were created to engage God's heart, not just to take care of His world, keeps us involved in the part we've been given to play.

I remember the time in my life when this truth became most real to me. For months I had been dodging a project I knew God wanted me to do. As I faced the risks involved, I became increasingly anxious and afraid. Finally, in a fit of frustration, I cried out, "Lord, I want to do what You've asked of me, but I just don't know how. I feel alone and afraid. I'm afraid of failing You. And I'm afraid of being alone as I try to please You."

During the months of postponement and worry, I had gotten the notion that God wanted me to accomplish something for Him on my own, with my own meager resources and in my own feeble strength. Though I knew better, I began to see Him as a distant, demanding boss who had assigned a job too hard for me to do.

In response to my fear, God spoke these words to my heart: "Child, I understand. You don't want to do this alone—and neither do I. It's *fellowship* I'm interested in, not just results. I don't need you. In fact, it would be easier not to use you, but I want you with Me as this thing unfolds and develops. You don't have to bring special skill or expertise; just bring your heart. I want the force of your own passion for this project to mix with Mine, and out of that will come something that ministers to Me."

It was at this point that I began to glimpse what really matters to God. Relationship matters; interaction matters. God is not lonely. He is not needy. There is nothing about Him that requires "help" from outside Himself. Nevertheless, like any true father, He desires fellowship with His sons and daughters. Though He is in no way dependent upon us, He passionately pursues relationship with us. Love and interaction are a function of *who* God is, not His means of accomplishing a desired end.

Here on earth, relationships (for all the discussion and interest they generate) are often the means to an end for us; they are what we "have" while we "do" something else. We are surrounded by relationships, but driven by accomplishment.

God is the opposite. Though surrounded by His accomplishments, He has given Himself to relationship. Though not in need of interaction, He has chosen to pursue it. For God, fellowship *is* the goal.

Many a mother knows the dilemma of having her four-year-old offer to help set the table for important guests. Not wanting to offend, she weighs the odds. Will it be worth it? By the time all the spoons are painstakingly placed upside down on the wrong side of each plate and the napkins have been carefully crumpled, by the time she's swept up the spilled sugar and rescued the butter dish from the dog, will it be worth the time and effort? The goal is to have a decent-looking table. Will it even come close?

For God, these situations are fairly clear-cut. There's no one He's trying to impress; there are no other, more important guests—there are only four-year-olds. They are the guests, and sharing supper with them is the goal. The table is being set for them, not in preparation for some other group of more important people.

Every mother who's risked it knows the richness of the meal that follows the help of a child. In spite of how the table looks, regardless of how many things fell to the floor or spilled in the process, the meal they share is more than food—it is fellowship.

Something has passed between them. They have stumbled through a process together, a process the mom could have accomplished more efficiently and with less mess if she had worked alone. But the child was drawn to her side and allowed to touch the things that are precious to her. Little four-year-old smudges mark her favorite pieces of crystal and china. Large four-year-old spills decorate an otherwise spotless tablecloth. Smudging, smiling, and spilling, her child has entered her world and carried the things of her heart.

In this we see a small glimpse of the nature of God's heart toward us. We begin to see that it is not just the quality of our stewardship, but also the confidence with which we embrace Him as Father, that touches Him.

If we insist on seeing ourselves only as servants, or as hired members of an orchestra, our labor will be heavy, taxing, and far from Him. If we trust in our ability to function *for* God more than we do in His desire to live *through* us, we will be consumed by fear of failure. If, however, we take God at His Word and approach the furnace of His fellowship as His much-loved children, the entire arena of intimate interaction opens to us.

As ministers to God in this place, as His children who love to participate in His Music, we are given access to the secrets of His heart and made welcome to the wisdom of His written Word. He speaks and we are trusted with His thoughts. He charts a course and we are called to His side as those in whom He delights to confide.

Drawn ever more deeply into His confidence, we collaborate with God in His love for the world. We share with Him in His endless compassions and participate with His heart as He formulates His will. Confident of His interest, we speak. Convinced of His pleasure, we act. With complete God-centered abandon, we "draw near with confidence to the throne of grace" (Hebrews 4:16), letting our "requests be made known to God" (Philippians 4:6), knowing that in the marvelous, irresistible strategy of His love, God has every intention of honoring our desires as He accomplishes His own.

Part Two

THE REACH OF
THE HEART

"I will put My laws into their minds, and I will write
them upon their hearts and I will be their God, and
they shall be My people."

Hebrews 8:10

Six

THE WAY IN

*As exciting and terrifying as the notion is, it seems
a bit simplistic to speak in terms of a "furnace of fellowship." It seems naïve to suggest that all we have
to do is face our fear, pack our bags, and start off
"into the fire."*

*Though oddly childlike, it's true. There really is
a God of intense intimacy and love who wants our
fellowship. The Bible says so. There really are fears
to be faced, preparations to be made, and a road that
each of us must travel.*

ECAUSE WE ARE finite beings, we tend to be linear in
our thinking and consecutive in our movements. We
start and finish a book, begin and end our workday, and look
"forward to" and "back upon" any given event.

Time and production have become the measurements of
our progress. As we assess the success of our day, we think in
terms of having had enough time to accomplish our tasks or
having advanced near enough to our goals to warrant our rest.

We are process oriented. If we sculpt or paint, choreograph
or compose, we move through the many stages that creativity
requires. When we travel or move from one place to another,
we define a point of departure and focus on a point of arrival.
We proceed in increments of time and space, always viewing
the journey in light of our destination.

We would be naïve to think that God is just like us. I believe He is much more simultaneous and circular in His actions. He does not search for a beginning and an end to something; He *is* the beginning and the end. He does not examine an event from a time/space ratio, for He exists far outside time, and His purposes can be accomplished even as they are conceived. They do not have to happen in time and space before they are real to Him.

God does not, as far as we know, have a production schedule that He must meet. He does not require of Himself "two new galaxies before noon" or to "complete a new firmament by nightfall." That would be absurd. He *is* the noon . . . He *is* the nightfall. He carries the hourglass; we are the ones who must live within it. He speaks, and stars appear; with a word, worlds are formed. God is not trapped in time and process as we are.

How, then, can we approach Him except that He help us? How can the finite interact with the infinite apart from assistance? Sin curtails us. We move one step at a time. We must travel *to* places . . . even to the places of God's heart.

Paradoxically, we find ourselves needing to walk *with* God into the very presence *of* God. He is not subject to process, but because *we* are, He is careful to lead us. He reaches out to us, takes us by the hand, and moves us step by step into the furnace of fellowship.

God is good at this. He is patient. For all the fire of His holy nature, He is still a father with a father's heart, and He has taught many children how to walk. He has drawn entire nations along by the hand, and He will help us if we let Him.

OUR FIRST STEP toward the furnace of fellowship is a very simple one. In other, more elaborate religious systems, this step would seem too simple, too elementary, to be noticed. However, we must notice and discuss it here because it is foundational for our future intimacy with God.

The first step is this: We make a response to God. That is all. The ease with which we make our response does not determine its value. How *well* we do what we do is not what determines its worth. Whether we react to God with some magnificent gesture of devotion or with a minute, almost imperceptible flicker of faith is not the issue. God isn't trying to *grade* us—He's trying to *enjoy* us![1] He wants us to reveal our hearts as an expression of trust in His heart. This step of trust in Him is essential.

It is essential because we are drawn into the furnace of fellowship by a process of communicating with God. He speaks and we respond. He then responds to our response and soon the silken cord of conversation takes shape between us. It is to this cord that we cling as we make our way into the place of His presence.

Communion with God in the furnace of fellowship begins in conversation with Jesus here and now. In fact, throughout the Scriptures and the history of the church, the pattern is well documented: Those who have walked with God have talked with God. From Abraham, David, and Isaiah to Peter, John, and Paul; from Francis of Assisi and Brother Lawrence to Hudson Taylor—the list is long. Luther, Tyndale, Wesley, Finney, Fanny Crosby, Amy Carmichael, Andrew Murray, Watchman Nee, Karl Barth, Dorothy Sayers, Livingstone, Tolkien, Bonhoeffer, Tozer, Schaeffer, Lewis, Moody—to be complete, the list would have to be as long as history itself. Whoever they have been and however unknown or well publicized their lives, the millions of believers who have walked this earth in close fellowship with God have been in constant communication with Him as well. Their lives have been filled with responses to God.

I am convinced that if we were to crack open just the few lives listed above, in every case we would find a conversation with God. Written, sung, preached, or prayed, deep within each life would run the same silvery strands of that silken cord, leading step by step into the furnace of fellowship. Whether through desperate cries in times of crisis or through passionate praises and declarations of devotion, each life would reveal a series of uniquely patterned interactions with God.

Perhaps you could hear the echo of some of their words as you read through their names. "Wilt Thou indeed sweep away the righteous with the wicked?" cried an anguished Abraham as he braced for the destruction of Sodom (Genesis 18:23). "My heart is steadfast, O God; . . . I will awaken the dawn! I will give thanks to Thee, O LORD, among the peoples; and I will sing praises to Thee among the nations," sang the passionate David (Psalm 108:1-3). "Woe is me, . . . I am a man of unclean lips," groaned Isaiah (Isaiah 6:5). "Thou my everlasting portion," sang Fanny Crosby, "more than friend or life to me; all along my pilgrim journey, Savior, let me walk with Thee."

God is no respecter of persons. If we want to grasp that cord and take that journey, we can. If we want to walk and talk with God, we can. In fact, if we have repented of our sins and declared faith in Jesus Christ, then we are already on the threshold of the furnace of fellowship. As we genuinely embrace Jesus, God's Son, the door is flung open and we are called to enter.

Responding to the saving grace of Jesus is only the beginning of a lifelong journey. After that, we continue to take steps toward intimacy with our Savior. We faithfully respond to Him.

Daily, hourly, minute by minute, as we listen for God's voice and continue to answer with our own, we are drawn further into the great exchange of hearts that is our home. As we choose time and again to talk with God about all that we think and feel, He begins to weave a special, one of-a-kind interaction with us. Through good days and bad, while facing great victory and soul-searing defeat, as we choose to share with our Father the real "stuff" of our hearts, He reveals to us the substance of His own.

Step by step, conversation by conversation, God leads us into deeper relationship with Himself. Speaking to us from the Scriptures, He weans us from the general clamor around us and teaches us the language of His heart. He draws out our unique, individual responses and, using these responses, He ushers us into ministry — ministry to Himself — out of which all other ministry will emerge.

Seven

THE REALM OF RESPONSE

Even as a person's first, tentative baby steps are similar in structure to their more confident, striding adult steps, our first step toward fellowship with God is like every other step we will ever take with Him.

S WE DISCUSSED in the last chapter, our first step toward God involves responding to Him. Because this is the first of many steps we will take with God, and all our steps in some way mirror each other, two points emerge. First, whatever response we make we address *to God*. He is our focus and it is to Him we speak. As we move forward into the furnace of fellowship, we choose to respond specifically to God, not to the things around us or to the trappings of the church, not even to the "salvation message" —but to God Himself.

For all the simplicity of this thought, it is more slippery than it first appears. It is slippery because we are natural-born responders living in a stimulus-rich world. As such, we have a tendency to give away what belongs first and foremost to God. Caught in the daily whirl of interaction with those around us, we often find ourselves responding to the urgent demands of earth before we acknowledge the call of heaven. Though we were created to respond to God, we respond to the people and events around us instead.

This is not a new temptation. It is exactly the one Eve so disastrously gave in to. She was created to respond to God, but chose to respond to Satan instead. Adam was not far behind; he was created to respond to God, but responded to Eve instead.

The second element in responding to God is that it is *our* response. When we come to God, we seek to genuinely represent ourselves; we do not push something of someone else's in front of us as we make our way into His presence. We don't borrow from another person as we interact with God, for it is the genuine cry of *our* heart that He waits to hear.

This is difficult. As human beings, we learn by imitation, and we grow dependent on the ways of others in the process of our spiritual education. Without intending to, we ride the coattails of a clear-thinking pastor or passionate Bible teacher. In our desire to know God, we depend upon someone else's relationship with Him. Unfortunately, when we imitate another person's interaction with God, we risk suffocating our own.

For a while, my own communication with God was stifled by my attempt to imitate someone else. During my early twenties, a Christian speaker came to our church, and in one evening I was captured by the pure, childlike way she had of interacting with God. She delighted me by the candor and ease with which she responded to Him, even in the midst of a large crowd.

As if she were in her own comfortable living room, this enchanting woman told stories about Jesus, sang little songs, and spread sprigs of poetry around the huge auditorium. She told us of giving flowers and God's love to people who passed by her on the big-city streets of her hometown. She sang for us the same sweet, breathy songs that she sang to cabdrivers during traffic jams and shopkeepers on rainy days. With joy-filled spontaneity she recited the same poems that accompanied the hot-from-the-oven cookies she gave to the homeless people in her neighborhood. Her vulnerability and warmth amazed me. She loved everyone she met. She loved hungry cats and stray dogs, burly garbage men, and crabby meter maids.

Most of all, this gal loved children. Images from *The Sound of Music* flooded my mind as she told of buying ice-cream cones for all the kids on her block, singing to them while they ate, captivating their hearts with stories about Jesus, then dabbing at the chocolate smudges around their smiling mouths when they were finished. I was mesmerized.

Though at that time I had very few heroes, this woman seemed as close as I might find. She was utterly charming and completely genuine as she spoke of spontaneously living out, in the world of flesh and blood, a true and loving expression of Jesus Christ. In short, she embodied everything I secretly wanted to be. As I responded longingly to her open, winsome ways, I wanted God to make me just like her. Perhaps, I thought, if He would just work a major miracle, I too could sing to total strangers and befriend abandoned animals. Perhaps, in spite of my reserved and intense personality, I could stick flowers in my hair, dance through busy intersections, and quote poetry to people on noisy street corners.

As I thought about my life, however, it seemed like a real stretch. Reviewing my fairly predictable existence, I found this scenario unlikely. Though I loved kids, I knew there'd be no way to control the scruffy little toughs on my block if free ice cream were involved—I'd have been trampled and left for dead in front of the concession stand. The most significant poem I'd heard recently was the old Civil War epic "John Brown's Body," and—with my voice—it seemed safer *not* to sing to anyone driving a car or operating heavy machinery. We had woefully little in common.

Even so, I decided to try. I asked God to change me to be

like her. As soon as I said the words, I knew I had made a mistake; I felt something cold move into my heart and I sensed God's displeasure. I groped around for the familiar, comfortable cord of communication that I held onto for so many years, but in that moment my hands were empty. All I held was a mirage—a fading, unfulfilled image of someone else's time-woven interaction, and it had no substance or reality for me.

I learned something then that I have not forgotten. I learned that God will never help me become like anyone but Jesus. He will never lend His assistance to re-creating me in any image but that One. He knows that only the image of Jesus should invade and change us into who He created us to be.

It is not God's desire to dive-bomb and obliterate the original "me" that *He* created just so He can fill the empty, smoking shell with Himself. This is not the *Invasion of the Body Snatchers*. Nor does He intend to replace an obliterated me with a hard-edged mirror image of Himself that I wear like a sandwich sign around what's left of my neck. How deep would that image be?

His intention is more radical than that—more confounding and poignant. He plans a massive, lifelong D-Day invasion of my heart, bringing new life—*zoe* life (quintessential life, God's life)—and in the process, destroying that part of "me" that's loyal to the Enemy. If there is to be anything even remotely resembling France remaining when the war is over, infantry must replace the saturation bombing. This, I have found, is how God has worked with me. He has not dropped bombs on me from a safe distance. He's sent infantry to fight for His life in me. Day after day I feel the battle raging throughout the rocky terrain of my heart, but I know it's love that has brought me to this. Though bombs are faster and easier, His love wants *me* accounted for when the war is over.

God impressed upon me that He is so fiercely protective of my uniqueness that He is prepared to deal with an infinite number of my struggles and failures before He will allow me to become like someone else.

Rather than being the effective shortcut I had imagined, praying to become like someone else is like asking God to perform a spiritual abortion. He is jealous for each of us—who we are now and who we are yet to become. Each life and each cord of communication that sustains life is of great importance to Him; He is unwilling to see them severed.

In this age of rock stars, image brokers, and virtual reality, Jesus alone must shape the hearts of those who make up His church. God intends us to be conformed to *His* image and no other.

In the next chapter we will see this more clearly. We will see that God tenaciously, patiently sojourns with us as we struggle to offer Him authentic, heartfelt responses. Jesus strives with us for as long as it takes, because ultimately He desires us to come to Him *for* ourselves, *as* ourselves.

Eight

THE GOD WE CAN SEE

We often struggle in our attempts to respond to God because we have trouble finding Him amid all the clamor and confusion around us. One of the most acute longings of the human heart is to see for itself the God of the Scriptures. We want to see God and know that He sees us. We want to respond to Him in a way that is not distorted or obscured by our human frailty.

SOME YEARS AGO my family and I traveled to California to visit my husband's parents. During a layover in Denver, the jumbo jet we were on filled up quickly, as all around us passengers squeezed through the narrow aisles. Carry-on baggage was stuffed into the already bulging overhead compartments and jammed under every available seat. The flight was full—so full, in fact, that some families were forced to sit separately.

Just behind me sat a two-year-old boy with his dad. Unable to get a seat in the same row, the mother had been placed several rows forward and to the far right. At one point during the flight, the dad lifted his son above the back of my seat so that together they could see where his mother was sitting. "Say hi to Mommy," the father said. "See Mommy? Say hi to Mommy, Sam."

But Sam couldn't see Mommy. His tiny eyes couldn't find her in the sea of unfamiliar heads spread out in front of him. While he looked around in growing bewilderment, his dad continued to talk and encourage. A huge, fatherly hand took hold of one of his little arms and waved it in Mom's direction. Over and over the words were repeated: "Say hi, Sam. See Mom? Let's say hi to her! Do you see her? She's right there; now wave; tell Mommy you love her." Poor Sam still didn't see his mom, so he said nothing; his arm remained limp and his face continued to register a blank, searching stare.

Finally, just as the father was ready to give up, Sam caught sight of the side of his mother's face and his tiny chest released a sudden, explosive yell. Across the entire plane everyone could hear him calling, "HI, MOMMY! . . . HI, MOM!" His little hand began to wave furiously and his face went from blank bewilderment to frenzied joy. He saw her! He finally saw her amid all the unfamiliar faces, and his response was immediate and complete. Nothing had to be coaxed or persuaded out of him. In fact, he became so enthusiastic, yelling "hellos" at the top of his lungs, that the dad finally had to haul him down and distract him with a book.

WE OFTEN FIND ourselves trying to respond to a God we don't yet "see." We know He's there but we can't find His face, so our effort at response seems hollow and forced. We tend to feel bewildered and false if we're encouraged to move through the motions and "wave" in recognition of a God we're still trying to locate.

The fact that our response is important and appropriate is no longer the issue for us. Our problem is that we don't know where to aim it. We don't know what direction in the sea that stretches before us to send our signals. Meanwhile we're surrounded by people whose worship seems effortless and focused. Their easy enthusiasm seems to mock our own struggle for sight.

Few things are as frustrating and lonely as being in the midst of a group of excited, expressive people when we can't see what they're responding to. In college, I used to sit with a blind friend at basketball games and describe the action to him. We attended a small private college, usually locked in grim, greasy combat with another equally small private school. Because there was no professional sportscaster, I would do my best to keep up a running commentary.

My best was pretty sketchy. Surrounded by the ricocheting screams of several hundred college kids and caught up in the general hysteria of close competition, I would sometimes forget to report what I was seeing. Often, at the most crucial moments, I would stop talking altogether.

David would go wild. Though a patient person by nature, he could sense the suspense, hear the roar of the crowd, and smell the sweat of excitement all around him. Finally, his hands would grip my arm like a vise. "What? . . . What? . . . What's happening?!" he would yell above the crowd.

By the time I had regrouped and caught him up on the action, his response would have been out of sync. Even if I managed to keep him current with a quick, clear description of the game, his reactions were always muted and restrained. He had none of the spontaneous, explosive responses of the other fans, because he needed to hear me to know what was going to happen next. He couldn't afford to be too loud, because then he wouldn't be able to "see."

IT'S DIFFICULT FOR us to respond to God with fresh, fervent worship when all we have to go on is what other people are saying about Him. It's hard to be spontaneous and involved when we're straining to find Him through the filter of another person's words. Eventually, no matter how inspired the speaker, no matter how careful the commentary, we get impatient with reports of God's activity and want to see Him for ourselves. We want to throw off all the hindrances and get a glimpse of His face with our own eyes.

Like the little man Zaccheus in the biblical account,[1] we stand in the back of the crowd, eyes wide open, searching, but still unable to see. There are too many other people in front of us. We can sense the excitement and hear the reaction of everyone nearby, but Jesus is still hidden from us. There are so many other "seers" that block our view; we wish He would simply clear them away. We wish Jesus would use His miraculous power to cut a path through the crowd and bring us forward, but He does not.

Instead, as with Zaccheus, Jesus waits for our desperation to reach its zenith. He waits as we scurry around the perimeter of the crowd, jumping up and down, edging between the bodies in front of us, growing ever more weary of our inability to see Him. Patiently, He allows time for our hunger, our desire, to escalate to the point where we are willing to do anything to get a glimpse of Him. In short, He waits for us to find a tree and climb it.

Jesus could, of course, make things easier for us, but He usually chooses not to. Instead, knowing how important this season of desperation is, He allows ample time for its full, foundational work to take shape within us. He knows that time often helps us realize the extent to which our dependence upon other people has become a blocking, hindering force. The longer we try to draw from others what only God can give, the more disillusioned we become.

Eventually, we begin to realize that commentaries and

reports are a God-sent encouragement, but they were never meant to sustain us. We begin to understand that, however clear someone else's view of Him may be, we cannot rely on other people in our search for Jesus. We cannot pass through them in order to find Him. We must go up. We must meet with Jesus personally and respond to Him directly.

There are countless ways to do this. Scripture indicates that, though there is only one way to find the Father—through Jesus, His Son[2]—there are innumerable ways to find the Son. Though there is only one mediator between God and men,[3] only one "door" into the furnace of fellowship,[4] there are as many different pathways leading to that door as there are people wanting entrance.[5]

This is by design. There is purposely no single, approved route by which we must approach Jesus. There is no official protocol for entering His presence. No polite, civilized statements are required of us before we can say what we really mean, for it is honesty, not propriety, that interests Him. Jesus doesn't want the raw reality of our need obscured by proper etiquette; He's not interested in pretty manners that serve only as a smoke screen for our pain.

Instead He wants each of us to come to Him in our own way, with our turmoil in hand. He wants every synthetic, cosmetic device used to camouflage our hearts stripped away and left behind. Everything artificial must be abandoned in our quest for Him. If we are evil, He wants us to say so. If we are hurt, He wants to hear it. If, like His disciple Peter, we have already walked with Him but betrayed our knowledge of Him somewhere along the way, He wants us to face Him once again. Real failure, real fear, real unbelief, and real despair are what He conquered on the cross. These cannot resist Him, but our cover-ups can.

The extent to which we insist upon impressing Him or hiding from Him is the extent to which Jesus must pursue us to bring us toward truth. He doesn't want us trapped by shaded, half-exposed realities, for He must have access, by a free act of our will, to the true nature of our need. He must be allowed to see the actual depth of our distress and hear the clear cry of our heart. To this He will respond. To this Jesus always responds, asking only that our desire for Him be stronger than our pride. Our desperation and desire can make a way for us into His presence.

We see this played out many times in the Bible. On one occasion a lame man was so anxious for healing that his friends climbed to the roof of the house where Jesus was staying, tore it open, and lowered him inside. Another time, while Jesus was sharing supper with a Pharisee, a sobbing prostitute defied all social restraint by falling at His feet, washing them with her tears, and drying them with her hair. Yet another time, a desolate, bleeding woman (considered to be legally "unclean" because of her illness) broke Jewish law, joined the crowd surrounding Jesus, and touched His robe.

In each case, Jesus responded. The lame man was forgiven of his sins and healed,[6] the prostitute was forgiven of her sins and gently welcomed,[7] and the bleeding woman was afforded the relief she had sought for twelve long years.[8]

Time and again throughout the Scriptures, Jesus is shown responding to the deep desire of those who wanted to see Him for themselves and meet Him personally. The loving, active nature of His response is recorded in detail in His interaction with the hemorrhaging woman. Though He could easily have moved on without ever acknowledging her touch, Jesus stopped everything and went looking for her. He knew that He had been touched by someone's faith and He wanted to respond face to face. Jesus wanted to respond to the searching heart behind the grasping hand.

"Who touched my clothes?"[9] He asked, turning to search the pushing, pressing crowd.

"You see the people crowding against you . . . and yet you can ask, 'Who touched me?'"[10] came His disciples' amazed reply.

Jesus, though hemmed in on every side, knew power had gone out of Him; His eyes continued to search the faces of the crowd.

Finally, the trembling woman came forward. Overwhelmed with fear and expecting a public rebuke, she nevertheless explained what she had done. "Daughter," said Jesus tenderly, "your faith has healed you. Go in peace and be freed from your suffering."[11] Instead of reprimanding her for breaking Jewish law, Jesus blessed her for her great faith.

By addressing her so openly, Jesus publicly lifted from her the stigma of her sickness and the decade-long weight of her shame. Because Jesus gently and intentionally required that she stand out from the covering of the crowd, she was met not with excruciating exposure but with the healing protection of His unflinching gaze.

In the simple act of responding to Jesus' call to come forward, this frightened woman stepped past the dark, tight places of her own soul into the vast arena of His acceptance and love. From this vantage point, she could see Jesus for who He really was, not as a quick-fix healer but as Messiah and Lord— not just as one who touches the body but also as the One who heals the heart.

This is the beauty of coming to Jesus as we really are: we begin to see Him as He really is. While requiring that we expose the true, undisguised nature of our need, Jesus reveals the true, undiluted strength of His salvation. He is the living

Word—the One who speaks as He heals. He is the God who does more than patch up the current crisis; He pursues the hidden, wounded places deep within.

This has always been His objective. Ultimately, it is the cry of the human heart that Jesus seeks to meet. In order to do so, He requires that we break free of everyone else's reports and admit our own need. He asks that we leave the covering of the crowd and come to Him as we really are.

When we come to Jesus openly and without pretense, we are never rejected, never ignored. Lame men and madmen, Roman soldiers and Samaritan women, harlots, lepers, and criminals—all were loved and received; all had equal access.

IT IS THE same today. Two thousand years later, Jesus' message remains passionate and clear: "Come to Me," He cries, "all who are weary and heavy-laden, and I will give you rest. Take My yoke upon you, and learn from Me. . . . For My yoke is easy, and My load is light" (Matthew 11:28-30)!

Regardless of who we are or what we've done, there is no exclusive, "correct" way to come to Jesus. All that is required is that we come in person and bring our weariness with us. There is no single, approved approach. Whether we limp in empty-handed or struggle under a load of our own accomplishments, this one thing is necessary: It must be our own desperation that propels us forward and the draft-force of our own desire that draws us to His side.

In this way our journey is never exactly the same as anyone else's. The path of our own search provides us with a living record that no one else's life can duplicate. Each of us is precious to Jesus, and it is often what we experience *as we seek Him* that begins to forge our individual history with Him.

I believe that our search is as valuable to Jesus as it is necessary for us; for in it He celebrates those things about us that set us apart from all His other followers. From the very onset, He nurtures the unique, even quirky, characteristics of the disciple He has called each of us to be.

It is with this in mind that Jesus waits patiently for us to find our "tree" and climb above the many human explanations that surround us. Jesus waits for us to move out on a limb that exposes us to His scrutiny even as it allows us an unobscured view of Him.

Then, just as with Zaccheus, everything beneath us becomes quiet. Jesus stops the chaos and confusion of the crowd and turns to look at us. He knows we're there. Now His gaze locks with ours and we see Him smile. Walking over to us, He speaks. He speaks and we respond, not to someone else's voice but to His! Not to a description of Him, but to Him!

"Make haste, child, and come down," He says, "for I must stay at your house today." The force of our own reaction surprises us. We become aware of ourselves responding with all the exuberance of a small boy finding the face of his mother in a crowded airplane. Suddenly, out of nowhere, comes a voice calling, greeting, *responding* . . . and it is our own.

All at once, worship has made room for us, for Jesus has come to *our* house. He has dined with us and now we are "responders." We have shared supper with Him, and we are no longer hungry.[12] We have talked together and now there is nothing forced or false about our show of affection. Jesus has come to where we live, and now the wave of our hand in worship is *our* wave, *our* welcome, to the God we can see.

Nine

THE REACH OF THE
HUNGERING HEART

"I, the LORD, am your God. . . . Open your mouth
wide and I will fill it."

Psalm 81:10

AVING EXAMINED OUR desire to see God, we must now address a frequent concern. It has long been considered more spiritually mature to "believe without seeing." The well-known and much-quoted verse "Blessed are they who did not see, and yet believed" (John 20:29) is often used to reward Christians who are willing to forego any sight of God. This, I believe, is a mistaken understanding of the verse and endorses an unnecessary poverty.

The context of this verse is that Jesus, upon His return from the grave, faced the skepticism of His disciple Thomas. To offset the doubts in Thomas's mind about the validity of His resurrection, Jesus showed him the nail prints in his hands and allowed him to touch the damaged flesh of each wound. This is what it took for Thomas to believe. He needed proof.

It was at this point Jesus uttered the now-famous words praising all those who would, through the centuries, believe in His resurrection without being shown the proof of nail holes and scars. But there is a substantial difference between a person needing to see God *in order* to believe and someone wanting to see God *because* he believes. The former is a requirement of the mind; the latter is what I call "the reach of the heart."

THE SCRIPTURES INDICATE that the seeking, reaching human heart has always delighted God. The eager, tiptoe stretch of a person's soul has always captured His attention — it is not a posture He ignores or denies.

Embattled old Job is one of the Bible's best examples of a stretching, questing, *reaching* heart. Though usually remembered as a forlorn figure in search of relief from his many sufferings, he was actually a strong, passionate, faith-filled man struggling for a glimpse of his God.

Job was a man who walked with God and was greatly blessed by Him long before he ever "saw" Him. So faithful a servant of the Lord was he that his reputation eventually reached hell and piqued Satan. A rare wager was made and it was agreed that Job's trust would be tested.[1]

Stripped of his family, health, possessions, and power, Job groped through the resulting darkness for the face of the God he loved. Friends, convinced that his circumstances were God's judgment for hidden sin, spent long days trying to lead him to repentance.

In time, Job became weary of their help and exhausted by their admonitions. His raw, grief-stricken heart was sick with fatigue and oppressed by the endless flow of their words. Blasting past all of their well-intentioned arguments, he finally cried out in protest. Pushing against every earthly constraint, his heart broke loose, rose up, and stretched toward heaven. Job cried,

As for me, I know that my Redeemer lives.
    I will see him for myself. Yes, I will see him with
    my own eyes, *I am overwhelmed at the thought!*
    (*Job 19:25,27,* NLT, *emphasis mine*)

Amid the growing cacophony of human voices all around him, Job cried out to God. Love and desire for the One he had served for so many years consumed him. A desperate resolve took shape within him and it became *God's* voice that he determined to hear, *His* face that he had to see.

In great torment of soul, Job continued to cry out for many days. Questioning, summoning, even challenging God to show Himself in person, Job's desperation made him brave; his pain made him bold.

If only I had someone who would listen to me and try to
see my side! Look, I will sign my name to my defense. Let
the Almighty show me that I am wrong. Let my accuser
write out the charges against me. I would face the accusa-
tion proudly. I would treasure it like a crown. For I would
tell him exactly what I have done. I would come before
him like a prince. (Job 31:35-36, NLT)

God responded. In one of the Bible's most profound passages, He comes to Job in the midst of a storm and speaks to him personally. God answers the cry of His servant with a cry of His own:

"Who is this that questions my wisdom with such ignorant
words? Brace yourself, because I have some questions for you,
and you must answer them.
    "Where were you when I laid the foundations of the

earth? Tell me, if you know so much. What supports its foundations, and who laid its cornerstone as the morning stars sang together and all the angels shouted for joy?

Have you ever commanded the morning to appear and caused the dawn to rise in the east?

Have you explored the springs from which the seas come?

Does the rain have a father? Who is the mother of the ice?

Can you stalk prey for a lioness and satisfy the young lions' appetites as they lie in their dens or crouch in the thicket? Who provides food for the ravens when their young cry out to God as they wander about in hunger?

"Do you still want to argue with the Almighty? You are God's critic, but do you have the answers?"
(Job 38:2-4,6-7,12,16,28,29,39; 40:1-2, NLT)

One hundred and twenty-six verses record the intensity and breadth of God's response to Job. Stanza by stanza, like laser surgery on a spiritual cataract, God's words carried the razor-sharp edge of His invasive light, cutting, piercing, stripping away the layers of Job's blindness and fog.

These words, though harsh, did not kill Job—they freed him. Though severe, they did not destroy his resolve; instead, they increased his faith. Clearly designed for the heart of a servant who needed assurance of his Master's sovereignty, they restored to Job a sense of God's passionate involvement in and concern for His creation—of which he was part. They were special words, burning words. Ripping through the bondage of blindness, they set Job free. With absolute accuracy they hit their mark and opened for him the eyes of his heart.

In response, a dazzled, humbled Job exclaimed,

"I know that you can do anything, and no one can stop you. You ask, 'Who is this that questions my wisdom with such ignorance?' It is I. And I was talking about things I did not understand, things far too wonderful for me.

I had heard about you before, but now I have seen you with my own eyes." *(Job 42:2-3,5, NLT, emphasis mine)*

The secondhand reports were over. Job had seen God. The depth of his anguish had driven him far beyond the pleasantries of protocol and, reaching for his beloved Master, Job laid hold. God felt the wild, desperate grasp of His faithful servant's hand and rewarded him with new sight. Though singed in the process, Job finally came face to face with the living God.

God was not angry with Job. His rebuke was not rejection. He did not rebuff Job with a flick of His finger and disdainfully shake free of a pesky human's pursuit — He honored him.

Something very important happens here. Though God silences Job, He does not push him away. Again, His rebuke is not rejection. In fact, the very whirlwind of words with which He corrected Job was the answer to his anguished cry. God knew Job wanted *Him,* not just his own reputation cleared — so He gave Job both.

To the three friends, however, for whom being correct *about* God seemed to outweigh any desperation *for* God, God revealed nothing of Himself, nothing of His splendor. He just said, "I am angry with you . . . for you have not been right in what you said about me, as my servant Job was" (Job 42:7, NLT).

SOME OF US, like Job, have walked with God for many years. We have believed in Him and served Him faithfully, but God has yet to feel from us the untamed, unrestrained reach of our hearts in search of His.

In our desire to be pleasing to Him, we have tried hard to behave well. We have concentrated on being very careful and very good. We have been "good witnesses" and "good stewards," "good Samaritans" and "good examples." We have been good at just about everything, except letting God feel the tough, tenacious pursuit of a hungry heart.

There's a reason for this. Many of us are afraid of overstepping our bounds—of disturbing God with our desire for Him. We are afraid that even if we call, God will not answer, that even if we reach, He will not respond. As pleasing as we have tried to be, we secretly assume that it will be someone else who gets the "real" response of His voice or the clear view of His face. In fact, because we know ourselves so well, most of us are privately convinced that we will be the one sure exception to God's willingness to interact.

In light of this, it can seem appropriately selfless, even Christlike, to view personal interaction with God as intended for someone else's more worthy life or aimed at someone else's more legitimate need.

Not so. Jesus' own need to see His Father was real and well documented, and He admitted it freely—"the Son can do nothing of Himself, unless it is something He sees the Father doing" (John 5:19). He would emerge from long midnight talks with His Father and declare, "Whatever the Father does, these things the Son also does. . . . I and the Father are one" (John 5:19; 10:30). Jesus was never ashamed of His dependence nor shy about openly expressing it.

There is nothing remotely selfless or Christlike about not needing to see God. There is nothing admirable about assuming that someone else is more deserving of what we *all* have equal access to.

Jesus calls us by His own example to be passionate and

jealous for our birthright. We were born to see God and to respond to Him. God has called us and saved us; now we must believe that He is also willing for us to see Him as He really is.

I REMEMBER A time in my own life when, after a long period of struggle, I knew what it felt like to reach for God with all my heart. It was a hard time for me. When it was over, there wasn't much left of my demure, civilized self. I had become so hungry for a glimpse of Him, so ravaged by my need, that what was appropriate behavior didn't seem to matter anymore.

For a period of months, I had been struggling to under-stand what I was reading in the Scriptures. Each time I opened my Bible, I felt I was reliving a scene from a Dickens novel. In my mind's eye I would see myself standing outside on a cold, snowy night, looking through a window into a warm, fire-lit room filled with feasting people. They were all sitting at a long, wooden table, eating from bright, colorful plates, and drinking from fat, full mugs.

Around the table the conversation was rich and lively with laughter, as Someone I could not see told stories and passed plates heaped with steaming food. Everything inside the room seemed light and warm. Everything outside felt dark, cold, and utterly removed from life.

Throughout that period in my life, whenever I opened my Bible to read, I saw this scene and felt anew all the same hunger and loneliness it represented. I would read but not understand. I would study because I knew there was substance to be had, but would always leave empty-handed. Everything I craved was locked behind glass in a room I could not reach.

This went on for a very long time. Long enough, at least, for me to adjust to the hunger and cold and to make an uneasy peace with being outside instead of in. I became a "watcher," an observer of all that others automatically considered their portion. While they were partaking, I was being "patient"; while they were wrapped in the warmth of fellowship, I cloaked myself with the cold. Finally, the day came when my bit of peace was shattered and the whole experience became too much for me.

The scene as I saw it that day remained unchanged, except that it seemed there was extra food being served—too much food for the number of people present. Plates were piled high, and the overflow that no one had space for was in danger of falling to the floor.

It was then that my heart broke and I began to cry. A deep, savage agony rose up within me and I cried out: "What about *me,* Lord? Don't You see my hunger and my pain? Don't You see that those scraps alone would be enough for me? They would be more than enough for me! Why are You letting them be wasted? I *need* them. Please God, please let me in!"

The page of Isaiah that I cried on was messy with ripples and streaks before it was all over. I remember sitting for a very long time staring at one verse in particular, as if it were a locked door. I cried repeatedly: "Whatever it takes, let me understand Your Word! Let me sit where You are and hear Your voice; let me see Your face with my own eyes! Please, God!"

When I finally got up from the jumble of paper and tears, a free, airy sort of emptiness blew through my heart, for I had dumped its contents right at the feet of Jesus. It was all out, and I knew He had heard me. My mind, frustrated by months of wrestling with hidden truths, had finally made way for my heart to speak. And, in response, Jesus released to the reach of my heart what He had been reluctant to give to the mere grasp of my mind. My patience had dissipated and in its place was a driving resolve that propelled me forward.

After that, I never again saw pictures of myself separated and alone when I read the Bible. Instead I heard things. I heard the clanking of dishes all around me; I saw plates being passed and heard stories being told. I still didn't fully understand Isaiah, but I wasn't standing outside in the snow, either. I was sitting inside at a long table by the fire and Someone, who I could now see quite clearly, was passing me plates full of food.

Lest this seem like a too-quick, too-magical account of intimacy with God, please know that I have told only the end of what was a major battle in my life. There were no quick solutions for me. Jesus let me struggle long past what I considered a healthy cutoff, but that's what it took for my heart to break free of its natural restraint and reach toward Him.

Looking back to that time, I can testify that there was nothing arbitrary in God's dealings with me. I believe He intentionally put those pictures in my mind to show me myself. Growing up in the church as I did, many things concerning the Scriptures came my way too easily. Much of what I lived on came through other people after they had done the hard work of studying the Bible for themselves. God had to force me to grow up—and He chose hunger to do it.

WHENEVER NECESSARY, GOD wields spiritual hunger as a weapon, and He does it purposely. He created us with an appetite for Himself, knowing that He alone can satisfy us. Yes, He intends to use us in each other's lives, but ultimately, it is His hand that feeds us. He insists on presiding over His own table and presenting us with the truth of who He is face to face. Now, as always when feeding His disciples, *Jesus* breaks the bread, *He* serves the cup, and it is in His presence that we eat and drink our fill.

If we truly desire to see God, if we long to hear His voice and see His face, He will help us. He will work with us and do whatever is necessary to cut away the layer of fog that obscures our sight. Through the wisdom of His Word, God will free us to see Him ever more clearly and, having seen, to respond more fully. If we ask, He will do it. If we are honest about our need, He will act.

In the next chapter we will see that the "reach of the hungering heart" is not all there is for the Christian. There is more. God has given us the ability to reach to Him in a ministerial fashion that has a powerful impact upon His heart.

Ten

THE REACH OF THE
MINISTERING HEART

*Hunger for God and personal desperation play a
vital role in driving us deeper into relationship with
Him. Even so, our hearts were designed to do more
than simply quest after God. They were designed to
ultimately find Him, enter into fellowship, and, from
that place of fellowship, minister to Him.*

*I*N THE TWO preceding chapters we explored what I call
the "first reach" of the human heart toward God. The
hallmark of reaching for God in this way is a profound sense
of personal need and a willingness to express that need honestly
and openly.

There is also what I think of as a "second reach" of the
heart. This is an equally aggressive action that is born of gratitude and love, not just of hunger and need. It is a response that
ministers to God in a special way because it is not motivated
by the desire to escape from pain but by the desire to have an
impact upon His heart. It is a reach for God Himself, not just
for the relief He can give.

Our hunger, blindness, and desperation are essential in
bringing us closer to God, but they can never cause us to love
Him. They can motivate but never inspire. They can dispel

complacency and drive us forward but never force us to trust.

An old, word-of-mouth story about Abraham Lincoln tells of a time when he visited a slave auction. Observing the proceedings from the rear of the crowd, his attention was caught by a strong, defiant, young slave girl with sharp, angry eyes. Something in her manner pierced him; the sheer intensity of her gaze spoke to him of the anguish of her captivity and her longing for freedom.

When it was her turn to step to the auction block, he and several others bid. With each rise in price, her hostility grew. Finally, Lincoln won, paid the money, and had her brought to him.

She came, rigid with resistance, arms tied behind her back, leg chains dragging.

"Untie her," Lincoln said.

"Oh no, sir!" her auctioneer responded, pulling her forward with a jerk. "She be a wild one! Ain't no end o' trouble in her. Ya best git her home afore ya be takin' her chains off." With that, he secured her to the horse rail, turned, and left.

Lincoln stood quietly for a moment, looking at the young woman. "What is your name?" he asked.

She did not respond.

"What are you called?" he repeated.

Steeling herself for the inevitable blow, she set her jaw, stared at the ground, and said nothing.

Taking the bill of sale from his pocket, Lincoln read it carefully, then marked the bottom with his signature. Slowly he stooped, undid the clasp of her ankle irons, and untied the rope that had cut into her wrists.

"You're free to go, Sara-Jane," he said, handing her the document. "You are free to choose your own life now."

Reaching again into his pocket, he drew out a card and

several coins. "If you have any trouble," he said, "call on me at this address and I will help you."

As the reality of what she had heard seeped slowly through her brain and into her muscles, the young woman grew weak and unable to sustain her rage. Minutes ticked by as anger gave way to confusion, and confusion to disbelief. Like someone in the grip of a personal earthquake, shockwaves of agonizing hope rippled through the muscles of her face. As she fought for control, her jaw clenched, then settled again; her muscular shoulders convulsed, then were still. Finally, a large, work-callused hand rose to take the papers and the money. Instantly, she turned and ran.

Lincoln watched as she disappeared down the rutted road. Taking the reins of his horse, he began to mount when he saw her suddenly stop.

Some distance away, she stood totally still. More minutes passed. Then, slowly, deliberately, she made her way back. Standing in front of him, she handed him the money.

"I choose you," she said, looking up for the first time into Lincoln's gaunt, craggy face. "You say I choose my own life now," she continued haltingly, ". . . that I work for who I want. You give me papers to show that I be free." The deep sinkholes of her oval face were wet with emotion. "If that be true . . . if I be free . . . then I choose you."

Whether fact or fiction, this story illustrates someone's free choice toward relationship even after her need had been met. It is, I believe, a good example for those of us who follow Jesus because, in the same way, it is ultimately our pursuit of relationship, not just rescue, that ministers to God.

WHEN WE MINISTER to God with the second reach of our heart, we willingly enter the realm of relationship. We acknowledge something between us that is deeper and more binding than a simple acceptance of assistance; we do more than think nice thoughts about the person who has helped us—we choose to rise and reach again.

After healing the ten lepers who had come to Him for help, Jesus experienced the second reach from only one of the ten. All ten men rejoiced in their newly found health, all were excited and grateful, but only one returned to Jesus and thanked Him personally. Only one pursued the source of his healing and intentionally reached again.

This is the nature of the second reach, that our focus shifts, our gaze gains altitude, and we return not only to receive from the hand of God but also to touch the heart of God. In so doing, we acknowledge that we can have an impact upon God, not just He upon us. We recognize a dynamic between us that is more personal and emotional than "need expressed—assistance received—thank-you note sent." We acknowledge that, by virtue of Jesus entering our world, God inaugurated something more relational and "risky" (for Himself) than if He had come as a one-way rescue operation. By entering our world to become like us, Jesus signals His desire for reciprocation. He longs for us to embrace His world and become like Him.

IN THE STORY of the prodigal son, we get another glimpse of this truth. As the younger, rebellious son of a wealthy merchant returned home starving, exhausted, and penniless, having spent much of his father's fortune, his father met him on the road and welcomed him even before the son could speak his words of repentance. So full was this father's forgiveness that, before the young man had finished begging for mercy and a place of servanthood, the father joyfully received him back as a son.

His father's own robe was flung around his shoulders; his father's ring was placed on his finger; and new sandals were put on his feet. Servants were then sent scurrying to prepare a grand feast of celebration.

If the story had continued to follow this young man, I imagine we would have seen another dynamic take place in his heart. I believe he would have made the second reach of the heart.

This time he, like his older brother before him, would be called upon to share in the full responsibility of relationship with his father. He would feel compelled to reach, not to quell the inner urgency of his own desperation but because—with his father's robe on his back, ring on his finger, and blessing on his head—he was a living expression of his father's forgiving heart. He was a recipient of, and therefore a representative of, his father's all-embracing nature.

In rising from his position of repentance and choosing to reach again, he would become the beneficiary of something even more loving, more binding, more extravagantly inclusive than a rescue operation. No longer would he be allowed to see himself as a tail-between-the-legs prodigal, but as a fully responsible partner in his father's household. However unworthy he felt, he would be caretaker and *partaker* of his father's wealth—a trusted participant with him in managing all the father held dear. Such is the nature of the exacting grace by which we stand. We are called as sons, not just servants; we are called to celebrate, not just survive.

I HAVE EXPERIENCED the progression of events that I've just described. In fact, it has stretched over the many years of my walk with the Lord. As explained in earlier chapters, I have felt the kind of driving need that cries out for rescue and relief. And

I have known the equally relentless pull of the Holy Spirit urging me to pursue more than just relief.

Though I have never made my way down the aisle of a Billy Graham crusade, I have, in times of personal crisis, sung the words of that same wonderful old hymn as I walked the aisles of my own heart:

> Just as I am, without one plea,
> But that thy blood was shed for me,
> And that thou bid'st me come to thee,
> O Lamb of God, I come, I come.
> (Charlotte Elliot, 1789–1871)

When I have come to God with these words, I have sensed His acceptance of me. Just like scruffy little Zaccheus and desperate old Job, my own scruffy, desperate heart has been heard and answered. Just like the tired young prodigal, God has responded to my reach toward Him and I have been accepted and loved.

I have, however, at the very moment of God's acceptance, also been challenged to rise and reach again. Even as I hear the Lord saying, "Yes, child, come to Me just as you are — broken, needy, and riddled with weakness and fear," I hear these words: ". . . and then let Me come to you just as *I Am,* complete in My strength and sufficiency, majestic in My power and provision. Yes, come in your weakness but then make room for Me to come in My strength; come to Me with your sin and grief, but then make way for Me to come to you with the fire of My forgiveness and joy!"

By simply expressing the desire to be accepted by God unconditionally — just as I really am — the challenge comes for me to accept *Him* unconditionally — just as *He* really is.

Suddenly, it is not enough that I receive comfort. Instead I am being asked to reach up and receive Him, the God of all comfort. It is not enough that I find answers to my questions, healing for my hurts, and forgiveness for my sins. I have been called into relationship with Jesus and it is clear that, as I rise and reach again, it will be to receive the fullness of all that He is—not just the benefits of all that He does. Like the prodigal, I respond out of sonship, not just servanthood.

INITIALLY, THE SECOND reach seemed daunting to me. I haven't always known how to make way for the Lord to come to me just as He is. In fact, it has taken more faith for me to receive God in all of His glory than it has for me to trust that He will receive me with all of my failure and sin. After all (I say to myself), He is God and all things are possible with Him. But I am only frail humanity. How can I hope to contend with the full force of His divine nature? How can even my huge hollowness of soul be space enough to harbor His manifest glory?

Instinctively, I know that if I make way for Jesus to come to me "just as He is," I will no longer be just as I am—I will be changed. I will no longer be in control of me—God will be.

This is a crucial point of reckoning—this is my hour of decision. Will I reach once, or twice? Will I pursue Jesus just long enough to feel better or will I stay and be changed? Am I going to opt for the cozy campfire of His presence or for the full, towering fire of His passionate nature?

The very act of staying in His presence, of reaching to Him again, ministers to God, because it invites His full influence in my life. It says that I want to be like Jesus and am ready to embrace the whole of who He is. It says that I want relationship, not just rescue. In the next chapter we will see how faithful God is in extending His hand to help us move toward relationship with Him. We will see that it is ultimately *He* who bridges the gap between the first and second reaches of our hearts.

Part Three

MINISTERING TO GOD

"My sons, do not be negligent now, for the LORD has chosen you to stand before Him, to minister to Him, and to be His ministers."

2 Chronicles 29:11

Eleven

FREEDOM TEACHER

There is a time of transition in the life of a Christian whenever God leads from the first reach of the heart to the second. Though this transition can be gentle and largely uneventful, for many of us it is a difficult, unsettling time.

It is a time when God challenges every former security and draws us, one bewildering birth contraction after another, into the world outside the womb of self-absorption.

ANNE SULLIVAN STOOD facing her employer squarely, her young head erect, her Irish jaw set. For a week since her arrival at the Keller home in Tuscumbia, Alabama, she had tried without success to penetrate her seven-year-old student's angry inner world.

Five years earlier, in February of 1882, Helen Keller had been stricken with a near-fatal illness. When her fever finally broke and the illness lifted, she had changed from a normal, active eighteen-month-old to a frightened toddler—completely deaf and blind.

Overnight her tiny body became a sealed time capsule for one of the most eager intellects of her generation. It would require a special teacher with a special kind of love to unlock all that now lay trapped within its sightless, soundless walls. Outwardly, Helen became a tyrant. Her family considered her so pitiful and in need of protection that no one was allowed to discipline her. In the name of love, her every whim was indulged and every foul mood tolerated. Left unchecked, her tantrums escalated until no one in the household dared deny her anything. Instead she was allowed to roam free of all restraint, groping from room to room, banging on walls when angry, toppling furniture when bored, and freely foraging for food when hungry. The older she grew, the more wild and dangerous her outbursts became.

One day, incensed that her newborn sister was sleeping peacefully in a cradle she often used for her doll, Helen rushed at the tiny bed in a rage and overturned it. Mrs. Keller caught baby Mildred just in time to save her life.

On another occasion, Helen discovered how to use a key, then locked her mother in the pantry. For three hours Mrs. Keller pounded on the door while Helen sat on the steps outside, laughing gleefully and enjoying the feel of the vibrations coming through the porch floor.

Eventually, the Kellers became convinced that a tutor was needed to help civilize their daughter. With the assistance of Dr. Alexander Graham Bell, they located Anne Sullivan and brought her to Alabama from Boston's Perkins Institution for the Blind.

SHORTLY AFTER HER new teacher arrived, Helen followed Anne to her room, slammed the door, locked it from the outside, and hid the key under the wardrobe in the hall. No amount of coaxing could induce Helen to reveal where she had hidden the key, so Captain Keller was compelled to get a ladder and help Miss Sullivan out through the upstairs window. Helen was delighted. Months later she produced the key.

This prank set the tone for the new student/ teacher relationship, and the two spent their first few days engaged in combat. The following excerpt was taken from one of Miss Sullivan's letters written just after her arrival at the Keller homestead:

> I had a battle royal with Helen this morning. Although I try very hard not to force issues, I find it very difficult to avoid them.
>
> Helen's table manners are appalling. She puts her hands in our plates and helps herself, and when the dishes are passed, she grabs them and takes out whatever she wants. This morning I would not let her put her hand in my plate. She persisted, and a contest of wills followed. Naturally the family was much disturbed, and left the room.
>
> I locked the dining-room door, and proceeded to eat my breakfast, though the food almost choked me. Helen was lying on the floor, kicking and screaming and trying to pull my chair from under me. She kept this up for half an hour, then she got up to see what I was doing. I let her see that I was eating, but did not let her put her hand in the plate. She pinched me, and I slapped her every time she did it.
>
> Then she went all round the table to see who was there, and finding no one but me, she seemed bewildered. After a few minutes she came back to her place and began to eat her breakfast with her fingers. I gave her a spoon, which she threw on the floor. I forced her out of the chair and made her pick it up. Finally I succeeded in getting her back in her chair again, and held the spoon in her hand, compelling her to take up the food with it and put it in her mouth. In a few minutes she yielded and finished her breakfast peaceably.

Then we had another tussle over folding her napkin. When she had finished, she threw it on the floor and ran toward the door. Finding it locked, she began to kick and scream all over again. It was another hour before I succeeded in getting her napkin folded.

Then I let her out into the warm sunshine and went up to my room and threw myself on the bed exhausted. I had a good cry and felt better. I suppose I shall have many such battles with the little woman before she learns the only two essential things I can teach her, obedience and love.[1]

The teaching of these two essentials was slow going with Helen. Obedience was actively avoided and every overture of affection rejected. Accompanying Helen's own reluctance to be taught was constant, though well-intentioned, interference from family members. Neither Captain nor Mrs. Keller could stand to see their daughter disciplined. Each time Helen lost a battle, she would run to her parents for sympathy and consolation.

NOW, SOME DAYS after her arrival, Miss Sullivan was still working hard to make her authority felt. It was at this point she approached the Kellers with her plan. She requested that she and Helen be taken to a small, empty cottage on the estate property and be left completely undisturbed until two weeks had passed. As difficult as it was for them, they made preparations for Helen to be handed over to the sole care of her teacher. It was agreed that during a two-week period they would not interfere in any way. They could visit and watch Helen from a distance but not let her know of their presence. Meals were to be brought to the cottage by the household servants, but even they were not allowed to touch Helen or let her know they were nearby. Only Miss Sullivan was allowed near her.

After her arrival at the cottage, Helen was outraged to find herself confined to a cramped space with only her bullheaded teacher. Her tantrums increased. Removed from everything most familiar, she became homesick, disoriented, and sullen. She was angered by any attempt at interaction.

This did not deter her teacher. In every corner of the cottage, Miss Sullivan's persistent hand came seeking Helen's tiny, rebellious fist. Relentlessly, it came, repeating over and over in sign language the names of objects in the cottage. Everywhere Helen went, she was required to listen to the silent, manual language of the deaf.

When Helen had a need and imperiously demanded that it be met, she was given the name of what she was demanding before her desire was fulfilled. If it was food that she wanted, she was force-fed the name of what she was eating, along with the food itself. If it was a toy she desired, first the name, then the toy itself, was given to her. Nothing was available to her just for the taking. If she had a need, she had to interact.

Helen grew increasingly frustrated at each new onslaught of communication. She shunned "the hand" that was moving in mysterious, incomprehensible formations. Repeatedly she pulled away and sank more deeply and dejectedly into herself.

As her homesickness grew, the battle raged around the clock. Day and night ran together as the student fought with increasing ferocity and primal wit. Finally, thoroughly exhausted, Helen's resistance crumbled and she succumbed to a hard-won under-standing—Miss Sullivan was in charge; she was not.

With this foundation finally in place, things went more smoothly. Helen became more compliant. Though she had no understanding of what she was doing, she learned to sign several words back into her teacher's hand. As yet, no connection existed for her between the doll in her arms and the word "d-o-l-l" that she could make with her fingers. The fact that everything had a name was still unknown to her.

Nevertheless, by the end of the two weeks Helen had changed remarkably. Miss Sullivan's letter of March 20, 1887, records her progress:

> My heart is singing for joy this morning. A miracle has happened! The light of understanding has shone upon my little pupil's mind, and behold, all things are changed!
>
> The wild little creature of two weeks ago has been transformed into a gentle child. She is sitting by me as I write, her face serene and happy, crocheting a long red chain of Scotch wool. . . .
>
> She lets me kiss her now, and when she is in a particularly gentle mood, she will sit in my lap for a minute or two; but she does not return my caresses. The great step—the step that counts— has been taken. The little savage has learned her first lesson in obedience, and finds the yoke easy.[2]

The Kellers were thrilled with their new, civilized little girl. Though much was left to be accomplished in the cottage, and Miss Sullivan begged for more time, the family insisted that Helen be allowed to come home.

The entire household celebrated her return with great rejoicing. In the cottage, Helen had learned many of the social refinements of a normal child her age. She sat at her place during meals, ate with silverware, and folded her napkin when she finished. She washed and dressed herself, combed her own hair, and picked up her toys. The experiment was a great success. Victory was clear—Helen had been tamed.

Miss Sullivan, however, was far from satisfied. This was not the end, but the beginning of her work. Obedience and the compliance it produced were not her final goals but the keys necessary to unlock prison doors. The bondage of Helen's raging rebellion had been broken but the capsule containing her heart and mind was still tightly sealed. Behind the vacant stare still lived a lonely, frightened little girl waiting to be found and freed.

Like a small landing between flights of stairs, Helen's polite, civilized behavior was only a place to rest and change direction before climbing higher. It was intended as part of a process—not her final destination.

So, day after day, teacher and student doggedly continued to pantomime the process of communication. Hour after hour their hands continued to move through seemingly meaningless gestures, waiting for the moment of flashing inner connection to come. It came on April 5, 1887:

> I must write you a line this morning because something very important has happened. Helen has taken the second great step in her education. She has learned that everything has a name, and that the manual alphabet is the key to everything she wants to know. . . .
>
> We went out to the pump-house, and I made Helen hold her mug under the spout while I pumped. As the cold water gushed forth, filling the mug, I spelled "w-a-t-e-r" in Helen's free hand. The word coming so close upon the sensation of cold water rushing over her hand seemed to startle her.

She dropped the mug and stood as one transfixed. A new light came into her face. She spelled "water" several times. Then she dropped on the ground and asked for its name and pointed to the pump and the trellis, and suddenly turning round she asked for my name. I spelled "Teacher" . . .

P.S.—I didn't finish my letter in time to get it posted last night; so I shall add a line. Helen got up this morning like a radiant fairy. She has flitted from object to object, asking the name of everything and kissing me for very gladness. Last night when I got in bed, she stole into my arms of her own accord and kissed me for the first time, and I thought my heart would burst, so full was it of joy.[3]

This event marked the beginning of one of the world's most famous friendships—and the lifetime of wondrous freedom it produced. Through the gift of communication, Miss Sullivan led Helen out of her confining darkness into the spacious world beyond.

She taught Helen to write English and to read Braille, then sent her on forays into the land of letters and books. Using words, Miss Sullivan carved for Helen's thoughts a passageway into the light, then watched as the light of other's thoughts reached her student also. She taught Helen sign language, lip reading, and how to speak, then ushered her into the richly patterned parlor of human conversation.

At the age of twenty-two, while still a sophomore in college, Helen astounded the entire educational community by publishing her first book. Two years later, in 1904, she did what no one thought possible: she graduated from Radcliffe—with honors.

After college this same girl, who as a child had groped blindly from room to room throughout her home, traveled extensively throughout the world. With her teacher by her side, she visited more than twenty-five countries, met with heads of state, and was decorated with numerous medals of distinction.

Ironically, Helen Keller, the wild little "savage" who had once taken such joy in locking her teacher in a room, had been *un*locked by her in return. Through a love stronger than her own stubbornness, she was released from the bondage of her body to become one of this century's most accomplished communicators. Over the course of her lifetime, Helen received global acclaim as a lecturer, author, and tireless humanitarian. Her twelve books and numerous articles have been translated into more than fifty languages, and the effect of her loving service on behalf of the disabled is still felt by millions worldwide.

All this was waiting on the other side of a cottage door. Though Helen could not have known it then, on the other side of disorientation and pain were freedom and new life. Great liberty followed the hated rigors of confinement, and the same hand that held the keys to freedom first tormented her with bitter, unrelenting confrontation.

In the cottage, the driving force of Helen's physical needs compelled her to break through to the first reach of the heart. Then, in the equally bewildering weeks that followed, her teacher built a bridge for the second reach of her heart that was yet to come. The cottage was not a place of punishment but of preparation; the weeks following were not spent polishing hard-won social skills but pursuing the language of life itself.

To any with a less-demanding love, the accomplishment of a quiet, correct life filled with proper behavior would have been enough. For many who knew Helen best, a tame, gentler child could easily have seemed like the pinnacle of success.

Helen's teacher was different. She wanted more. Helen's teacher wanted her *free!*

WE HAVE A TEACHER who wants His people free. Jesus wants more for us than tame, civilized behavior and the "shoulds" of the Christian life. He wants true communication, genuine heart responses—not just polished, robotic imitations of a reality we don't yet share.

For most of us, the path to freedom leads through The Cottage. In order to accomplish our ultimate release, Jesus often removes us from what is most secure and emotionally familiar. He takes us from the soft, indulgent arms that have become our home and sequesters us with Himself.

As we are locked in a strange, foreign place where everything is threatening and new, our Teacher waits for the real "us" to emerge. There in the face of our raw, screaming need and dark, rebellious anger, He begins to meet with us, unhindered by the kind of "love" for which comfort is more valued than communion.

When we are hungry, it is His hand that feeds us; when we are thirsty, it is He who gives us something cool to drink; when we are worn out from our tantrums, it is Jesus Himself who makes a place for us to rest. Everywhere we turn He is there, His hand in our hand, maddeningly, unrelentingly spelling new, mysterious words of life.

Most of us don't respond well to this place of disorientation and forced communication. We are angry and in pain. We don't recognize where we are or even why we're there. We just know that something has gone terribly wrong with our safe, familiar world. Perhaps our relationships are crumbling, our finances are failing, or our health is deteriorating. Maybe, after twenty years at the same job, our competence is being questioned and our worth reassessed. Those systems that were once our strongest means of identity and support are now just a point of painful, wistful recollection. Like Helen, we are frightened and homesick. We want to go back to being loved in the old familiar ways that allowed us to remain emotionally unchallenged and internally unchanged.

Once in The Cottage, however, we almost never come out unchanged. For most of us it is a profoundly transforming experience. If we enter as an unbeliever, it is not unusual to come to a place of faith in Jesus and experience His saving grace. If we enter as a nominal, passive Christian, we often emerge energized, active, and more committed to obeying God's Word and doing His will. If we go in as an already active, committed follower of Jesus Christ, we come out stripped of all our formulas for living the Christian life and newly dependent upon Jesus for everything.

Whatever changes The Cottage may produce in us, when we finally emerge, we are faced with yet another surprise. Like little Helen, we're amazed to find that for all the trauma we've just endured, our Teacher's work has only begun. In spite of our recent breakthrough (whatever it may be), the bewildering hand signals don't stop. Even though we're using all our newly acquired table manners and social skills, the lesson isn't over.

Because we don't understand the true nature of our Teacher's love, we underestimate the full scope of His plan. We often pass through our prison-like struggle still unclear about the goals of the One with whom we've been confined. We think all He cares about is that we "get saved" or become more productive, obedient disciples. We mistakenly assume that all the battles and mysterious hand signals have been for the primary purpose of making us more compliant at the dinner table, more presentable in public.

Unaware of the rest of our Teacher's agenda, we begin to rely on simple behavioral changes. We go to church, smile a lot, and say nice things. We read our Bible and witness more. We work hard at being helpful. We stay in our seat, eat with silverware, and fold our napkin when we're finished.

This makes many people happy. We're so much improved over the "old" us that the grand experiment is declared a success. Jesus "works"; we've been changed.

The only problem with all this personal improvement is that we have a Teacher who wants more—we have a Teacher who wants us *free!*

When Jesus closes The Cottage door and starts talking to us, it is not for strict behavioral and attitudinal change—it is for freedom. The words that Jesus spoke two thousand years ago are still true today: "If therefore the Son shall make you free, you shall be free indeed" (John 8:36).

Even after the moment of our salvation, even after we decide to embrace genuine commitment and active church involvement, even after we come to a point of total trust in Him—Jesus wants more. He wants us free to speak the language of the heart.

Jesus is not satisfied that we're easier to control and nicer to be around; He wants us free to converse and commune. He's not interested in holding us hostage by the sheer force of our own need; He wants us healed and whole. Jesus isn't even content that we've found in Him a place of security and shelter from the storms of life; He wants us free to venture back out into life's risky, loveless waters—taking His love with us as we go.

Jesus wants more for the adulterer than the relinquishing of a mistress—He wants him healed enough to embrace the intimacy of marriage. He wants more for the alcoholic than iron-willed sobriety—He wants her free to face life without emotional escape. He wants more for the troubled Christian than a white-knuckled wait until heaven—He wants him free to pursue all that the Father has put here on earth. In short, the person that the Teacher tangles with in the confines of The Cottage will not just be free of painful compulsions and a fear-filled future, he will be free to commune with the living God!

Jesus purposely takes us to The Cottage and battles with us there because, at the very point of our greatest wounding, He wants to give us words. He wants to give language to the locked places of our heart—to talk to us and to hear us talk back. His goal is to find and free the lonely, lost parts of us that were sealed by sickness long ago—to penetrate our inner darkness with light, our soul-silence with sound.

Whatever The Cottage may be like for us, this is its fundamental purpose. It is for freedom that we have been brought to this place of confinement and confrontation. Yes, our time there is often brutal and bewildering. It is, however, not a place to fear, for whenever we are with our Teacher we are under love's jurisdiction—and true love allows no haphazard destruction.

His searing heat wounds only in order to heal. He crushes, only to create anew all that was originally intended to be. His love defends while it disciplines, protects while it purifies, and invades the safety of the shell, only that the pearl may go free!

IF YOU HAVE ever been to The Cottage, you know that it is often in this place of pain and great struggle that Jesus begins to build the bridge that connects the first reach of the heart to the second. This is the scope of His plan. Ultimately, Jesus wants us free enough to rise and reach again of our own accord. He wants us able to say with Israel of old,

"Come, let us return to the LORD.
For He has torn us, but He will heal us;
He has wounded us, but He will bandage us.
He will revive us after two days;
He will raise us up on the third day
That we may live before Him.
So let us know, let us press on to know the LORD.
His going forth is as certain as the dawn;
And He will come to us like the rain,
Like the spring rain watering the earth."
(Hosea 6:1-3)

Just as Miss Sullivan rejoiced in a newly transformed Helen crawling into her arms at last, Jesus longs to feel the second reach of our heart coming to Him in full embrace. He wants to hear each of us say, "I will return to the Lord—yes, I will know, I will press on to *know* the Lord!"

Coming to Jesus in this way, with eager arms outstretched, tells Him that we are ready. Ready not only to be loved but to love; ready not only for rescue but for relationship. The second reach of the heart tells Jesus we are ready to explore with Him the vast world of His Father's kingdom, to follow Him to that place of fire and fellowship where everything has a name, where every symbol has substance and every movement has meaning.

There He will walk with us and talk with us. There, as the Scriptures say, He will abide in us.[4] With His hand in ours, Jesus will continue loving us, teaching us, *freeing* us—to learn the vibrant languages of His heart.

Twelve

THE COTTAGE

The whole life of a Christian is a holy desire. What
you long for as yet you do not see . . . by withholding
of the vision God extends the longing, through longing
he extends the soul, by extending it he makes room in
it. So, brethren, let us long because we are to be filled.[1]
Saint John of the Cross

*I*N CHAPTER 1, I told the story of my time in The
Cottage—my own experience with the Freedom
Teacher. It is significant to me that I was already a strong
believer when that crisis occurred. By my own estimation, I
was doing fine in my faith just before I plunged into that fif-
teen-month season of turmoil. Though I did not realize it at
the time, God Himself was struggling with me, and it was His
hand that freed me. It was God who created my crisis, who
dropped the questions into my heart and then, months later,
answered them.

Methodist pastor Dr. Thad Rutter Jr. speaks of coming to
this same conclusion while in the grip of his own Cottage experience. He writes, "The Bible jarred me into the awareness that
quests for God don't originate with the human mind and heart
but with God. Before we seek God, God has been seeking us.
Before we inquire of God, God has been inquiring of us. . . .
Before we long for God, God longs for us."[2]

So why does this God "who longs for us" make it so traumatic, so difficult to break through to the very thing He's determined to give us? Like making a kid fight his way past chained dogs and pits of steaming sulfur on the way to his own birthday party—why go to all the trouble of traumatizing us on the way in? Is it because we, like Helen Keller, are dangerous to others and resistant to Him? Are we fighting our Freedom Teacher as she did hers?

Pastor Rutter certainly didn't seem to be. As he entered his thirty-first year of faithful pastoral service to two churches, he seemed anything but a troublemaker. Even so, God was about to trouble him. He reflects on that season of struggle in his book *Where the Heart Longs to Go* by recalling,

> What happened was both quiet and of crisis proportions. I didn't lose my job, marriage, or anything else of significant value. On the surface, all appeared normal; I showed up where I needed to and did what I was supposed to do as a pastor. But that normal functioning belied a deep inner dysfunction . . . an underlying dissatisfaction and emptiness in my life and ministry.[3]

Neither would Father John Powell have fit the description of someone who needed a stint in The Cottage. As one of Loyola University's academic superstars, he has earned advanced degrees in the Classics, Theology, English, and Psychology. By the age of thirty-five he had toured and studied in Europe, learned three additional languages, and earned a doctoral degree, *magna cum laude*. Upon his return to Chicago, he maintained a demanding schedule as a popular public speaker, author, teacher, counselor, and parish priest. He could hardly have been considered a slacker who needed to be cornered and confronted. Nevertheless God did corner and confront him.

In his book *Touched By God,* Powell tells of his ordination, travels, intellectual accomplishments, career successes, and lecture circuit accolades—all ultimately leading to deep and bitter disillusionment. "The aroma of incense filled the air of my personal world," he wrote. "But inside me the crisis of being over thirty-five and needing a new and deeper meaning in life was forming like dark storm clouds. So you proved you could do it. Then you proved it again and again and again. Now where do you go? What do you do for an encore?"[4]

These two men were both Christians, scholars, and serious servants, yet both were hauled off to The Cottage for a spiritual showdown. Why? The job was getting done; they were a pleasure to be around; parishioners were getting their needs met—why mess with success? Why corral these two with the same trauma as someone who has to be physically restrained just to sit at breakfast? Don't compliance and accomplishment count for something with God? *Not if they stand in the way of freedom by serving the same purpose as violent behavior and open rebellion.*

Let me explain. I have come to believe that the trauma of The Cottage is never capricious or coincidental. It is carefully designed by God to hit at the very core of our deepest need. Far from being just a haphazard convergence of stressful, depressing circumstances with which God chooses to torment us, if we look closely, we can usually find a much more strategic and substantive coordination of pain. For instance, in the life of Helen Keller, it was in the realm of communication that she was most limited and isolated. It is more than coincidental, therefore, that it was in that very area that her teacher's actions tormented her.

By this am I saying that God purposely causes our suffering? No. I am saying that God is so sovereign that by whatever circumstances Satan may have intended our harm, He, God, is able to accomplish His own plan of higher good. God never wastes our pain. In His skillful, loving hand, the Enemy's dagger becomes a surgeon's scalpel. And, though He allows us to make evil choices, He is never outdone by evil itself. It has never been God's equal. Wherever evil seeks to destroy, God moves to restore—and it is often in the very presence of death that He brings us to newness of life in Him.

Dr. David Biebel, the author of two books dealing with pain and loss, uses this example to make sense of God's role in our suffering:

> My brother Paul, a general contractor, sees an anal-
> ogy between how he builds a house and how God
> builds us. When it's time to get underway, Satan—
> the excavator—digs a big, deep hole. The digging
> tears up the landscape, ruins the view, and generally
> makes a mess of everything. The excavator's plan is
> to throw us in and bury us. But when that hole is
> just the right size, God—who has been watching
> closely—steps in and says, "Okay, that's enough. It's
> just right." And He begins to pour the foundation for
> the dwelling He's had in mind all along.[5]

God is all-merciful and all-good. Because of this, He not only organizes the trauma of The Cottage to our greatest benefit, He also intentionally blocks our way of escape. Our Freedom Teacher, we find, has us in a new, strange place—and has barred the door. No longer can we get to the well-worn pathways of consolation and retreat. Suddenly, we can't jump higher, perform better, take the right pill, say the right thing, find the right job, pray the right prayer—none of it works for us anymore. We are cut off—trapped. We are sequestered with Someone we thought we knew but who suddenly doesn't seem very friendly.

Because the pain of The Cottage is so intentional and inescapable, it has the power to bring us to the end of ourselves. What we find when we get to the end of ourselves in this fallen world is usually some interwoven mix of the same two agonies: fear and shame. As complex as we like to imagine ourselves to be, this fairly basic duo is at the root of much of the human heart's struggle with pain and captivity.

Our fear often operates as the guardian of our shame and our shame gives our fear a focal point. Together they form that most notorious and vigilant of protective partnerships. They keep us safe from what we most dread: exposure of our deepest wounds. Protecting ourselves from exposure takes enormous energy. Fear and shame have enormous energy to give. They're almost 100-percent energy—they never rest. The arrangement is effective for most of us—even for careful, compliant Christians.

So it is that a true Cottage experience with God is always about something much deeper, much more costly and exciting than altered behavior. It is preparation for freedom and for the moment of meeting from which our freedom springs.

Over the years I have come to think of The Cottage not as a place, but as a season of time. It is to me a symbol of that period or periods of time in people's lives when they are being pursued by God in a definite, often difficult way. It does not always include obvious, external crisis, but there is usually the awareness that we have run up against the proverbial "brick wall." We are no longer moving forward at our own speed, our trusty set of coping mechanisms working for us as it once did. We are being challenged on a deep and often frightening level by something or someone we don't recognize and therefore don't trust. The survival of who we are and how we perceive life are clearly at risk. Energized by all the known comforts we have to lose, we resist bravely, cunningly. Like Helen Keller's, our initial "fight" is often fiercely primal.

But, as we eventually discover, in Jesus we have come up against someone even more cunning and creative. Matched stroke for stroke, maneuver for maneuver, we are ultimately left thoroughly depleted, wearily resigned. The Cottage therefore represents not just a season of time and turmoil but the initial fight we put up as God challenges the status quo of our life.

In The Cottage the Freedom Teacher purposely calls out our fear. He allows situations to occur that cause our deepest anxieties to rise to the surface. Then, with a steady hand, He traces the frightened, anxious thoughts to the shame and woundedness beneath.

DURING MY OWN months in The Cottage, God exposed my fear again and again. Fear of futility and helplessness seemed to dominate my days. My deep dread of being faced with situations for which I felt responsible but not sufficient made me ever more energetic and determined not to fail. That dread was traced to a distant street corner in the port city of Guayaquil, Ecuador, the summer my older brother, Scott, and I visited our missionary grandparents.

It was noon on the equator but my skinny, nine-year-old body didn't feel the heat. My hands had grown cold and clammy with nervousness. They clutched the small patent-leather purse hanging from my shoulder. Though I was surrounded by busy traffic and a lunchtime crowd, the street noise began to fade as I watched the stretched lips in front of me move: "Mira al pobrecito, seniorita. Pobrecito. Por favor." ("Look at the poor little boy, Miss, poor little boy. Please.) The mothers and their children formed a long, wavy line of bodies at my feet.

My grandmother and I had just rounded a corner when I saw the small huddle on the ground. At first I thought there was only one mother, one child. But as I came closer, moved along by the press of people, I saw them all. The bowls and the children and the tattered, drooping mothers covered the sidewalk. Every urine-encrusted strip of newspaper spread on the hot concrete held its own personal piéta. The children were lying in their mothers' arms quietly, oddly. Their limbs were askew. They didn't move and their tiny deformed bodies were patient with the flies that clustered at their runny noses. The mothers held on loosely — resignedly. None of the fierce, fighting motherhood of a well-fed, Western mom registered in their hollow eyes. Instead I saw an ancient wisdom. It was not wise to love too much in a place with too little to eat. Too much pain and too little time with the too-tiny body in their arms kept them sober and detached. Like actors in a silent movie, they looked at me and lifted their small, baked clay bowls.

Absurdly, my strongest desire at that moment was to hide my legs. They seemed to betray me and the ease of my suburban Chicago life. Though bony, they stood straight and strong beneath my cotton dress, and I felt the wise eyes looking at them and knowing me. Surely, even a child with clean, unscarred American legs tucked into neatly folded ankle socks would have money to put into small red bowls. But I didn't. I had nothing but a comb and a Kleenex. The purse was just for show. It was empty of anything that could help. I was empty of anything that could help.

As has happened to me at various vow-making moments in my life, everything around me seemed to grow dim and distant. Like looking through the wrong end of binoculars, the scene in front of me seemed to compress into one far-off, never-ending line of innocence and anguish. My ears filled with the sound of my own heartbeat and the outer edges of my vision turned gray and grainy. I stood transfixed by the need, clearly powerless yet clearly culpable. It was up to me. I was, after all, a Christian. I believed in Jesus and all His miracles—I, like Peter, should be able to give "such as I had" and watch things happen. So what if I didn't have money in my purse! I had Jesus, didn't I? I should give them *Jesus*—His touch, His healing, His happiness!

But I couldn't. I didn't have that much Jesus. I felt empty of what mattered to me most. The purse, the person . . . not enough, helpless, empty.

THOUGH I DO not remember it now, I'm sure my grandmother must have given some money, but my personal shame was not appeased. I had failed some kind of deep spiritual test, and the experience of that day haunted me into my adulthood.

It's strange that one three-minute event could have such a lasting, formative effect, but it did. I became a "giver," an eager doer of good deeds. Pain—everybody's pain—became my pain. The world and its needs became my burden—mine to champion, mine to carry. It was many years and a trip to The Cottage before I began to see the twistedness of my motives. My actions were good, but my motivation was fear. It was fear that energized my goodness, not fellowship with the God who *is* all goodness. Though it took me years to realize it, I was in a crisis of faith. Because of human suffering, I no longer felt too sure of God's goodness. *My* goodness seemed more reliable, more readily responsive. *If I were all-powerful,* I thought to myself, *I would have been more conscientious about being helpful.* So I came to God's rescue and became more helpful—*for* Him. In His name.

This subtle judgment of God's character seemed increasingly appropriate through the years as the daily newscasts on television gave the dead and wounded statistics for the Vietnam War. It also became a more entrenched pattern each time I chose to do things in my strength instead of His. Until The Cottage.

In telling his story, Rutter gives us insight into the earliest, most formative wound he can recall.

> At age fourteen, I was in a head-on collision that killed a passenger in our vehicle and seriously injured my father and me. My front teeth were smashed, and my left leg was shattered at the thigh. But toughest of all for me at fourteen was the stark realization that the safety net of my father's love could not protect me from the terror of death. I lived well into my adult years with this horror unresolved in my life . . . my foundations were severely shaken. The guilt and shame I experienced as an "unworthy" (or so I thought) survivor scarred me, and I carried deep doubt about my self-worth.[6]

Powell on the other hand, remembers the point in his early twenties—while still a novice studying for the priesthood—that began his gradual downward slide into spiritual crisis.

> The devil never asks that the first step be a big one. . . . It is my honest, retrospective judgment that

at this point I was beginning to seek, to want something more than God. And this is my idea and definition of delusion. I was confusing the less important with the more important; I was confusing the means with the end. Instead of preparing myself intellectually to help build the Kingdom of God, I was grasping for the success that would sustain my ego. I was competing for the identity or image of a "very bright" student. . . . My heart was a divided city. The tenacious desire to be a success as a student and as a teacher had seduced part of me, doubled my vision, divided my heart. These were, I fear, years of compromise; and a compromised seeker does not find the face or heart of God.[7]

SO WHY DO even productive, well-behaved believers end up in The Cottage with the door bolted behind them? Because even those of us who aren't causing God problems (or don't think we are) have a Teacher who wants us free. Free in the face of our woundedness and sin. This is the reality of the law of liberty: "Now the Lord is Spirit; and where the Spirit of the Lord is, there is liberty" (2 Corinthians 3:17). Jesus wants us free to truly know Him—and from that knowledge to reach to Him in fellowship, sure of His goodness and of our welcome.

So it's to The Cottage that we're taken. Those who go there are often already Christians; they already love God and serve Him, but have somehow lost touch with who He is along the way. Under the weight of good deeds and many deadlines, they let go of the only part of Christianity that really matters: Christ. And so, like Anne Sullivan, God ignores the applause of all who think good behavior means a good, free heart, and

He comes as the Invader, jealous for our freedom.

God does the healing work necessary in a peculiar way. He doesn't just expose the wound, He moves into it—to live there. This is His pattern. Jesus gave the lepers, harlots, tax collectors, Samaritans, and Romans—in fact any of the social outcasts and hated enemies of His day—the one thing no one else would give them: Himself. He came to their homes, their parties, their weddings. He healed their children and drank their wine. What did He do with untouchable people? He touched them. How did He behave with people whose touch the temple leaders said would defile Him—harlots, for instance? He welcomed their touch. Did He welcome them secretly? No. Openly, publicly.

Jesus is not only unafraid of what ails us; He has every intention of healing it. He does this by entering the place of our greatest shame and making it His home. That's what The Cottage is really all about. That's why it is so healing, so necessary. Just like Miss Sullivan as she worked with Helen, He fights us tooth and nail to get to the very thing we most want to hide—our anguished, silent aloneness, our terrible fear of the darkness within us. Then, once He arrives at the deepest part of our darkness and shame, He unpacks His bags and sets up His tent. He makes a fire and fries some fish.[8] He feeds us and talks to us. In the place of our deepest wounding, He gives us words.

As far as I know, Jesus is the only God who initiates this kind of proximity with people when they are in the grip of sin and shame. I remember watching a documentary about a two-man expedition climbing to the source of the Ganges River in India. In the course of their travels, the reporter and his cameraman passed through a village and met a man who had been standing on his feet for more than seven years. Hunched over, his elbows resting on the woven hammock slung in front of him, his bare, elephant-like ankles and swollen feet told the deeper story. He explained through an interpreter that this was his act of honor and sacrifice to the god of the Ganges. He hoped, in light of his many years of suffering and self-denial, that his god would receive him someday so that he could repent and be cleansed. The years of standing were just a preliminary for someday making an approach to his god.

As a Christian, I was pierced to the heart. As I watched this man's matter-of-fact awareness of his sin and the provision he was making for his acceptance, I began to glimpse the enormity of what Jesus has made possible for me.

Was this gentle Hindu overreacting? Not at all. He seemed to have a better understanding than I of the barrier our sin has created. What's different between us is the nature of who we worship.

In Jesus, I have found the one God that does the advancing, the initiating, the knocking, the pursuing. He comes *toward us* and purposely disturbs us enough so that we fully see what He has always seen about our true motivations. Then, just about the time we're getting out a good pair of standing shoes, we see Him setting up chairs, building a campfire, and beckoning us to sit. Talking together, the hours pass. Slowly, imperceptibly we let our weight down, slip off our shoes . . . and rest.

The real Jesus is stunning. So indifferent is He to the horror of His surroundings when He comes to us that no one would ever suspect the price *He* had to pay just to sit down in *our* presence without destroying us. Pay, He did, however, and having done so, He makes Himself right at home. He knows His "work" is finished. In fact, *everyone's* work is finished. That's the whole point. We have nothing but our faith to add to make

His communion with us a present-tense reality.[9]

Powell and Rutter have found their rest in God. They have entered in. Both of these extraordinary men have become beautifully simple and childlike in the presence of God—to this their lives testify. Daily they can be found talking to Jesus, listening to Jesus, celebrating with Him, and building with Him a sanctuary of rest-filled ministry to His heart.

This is what Jesus does with us after The Cottage, as we will see in the next two chapters. This is where we are headed. Over time, He helps us build a sanctuary on the very ground that once held our shame. It is in *this* place, the site of our most unfaceable fear, that He leads us into communion. As we will see in the next chapter, it is this very realm of former devastation that He has chosen for His own invasive undoing of us and His happy, tender enfolding of us. And it is here that He calls us to rise and reach to Him again.

Thirteen

THE MOMENT
OF MEETING

As I wander through the dark, encountering diffi-
culties . . . I sense a holy passion pouring down from
the springs of Infinity. I thrill to music that beats
with the pulses of God. Bound to suns and planets by
invisible cords, I feel the flame of eternity in my soul.[1]
Helen Keller

WHEN ANNE SULLIVAN and Helen Keller left the cottage
together two weeks after they had entered, they were
not friends. Neither were they still at war. They left with a
clear and mutual understanding of who was the victor and
who was the vanquished, but that is all. Miss Sullivan had won
the obedience of her student but not the affection. Helen,
though tame and apparently content, would do what was
required but nothing more. She repeated finger movements
that meant nothing to her except that they produced the
things she needed: food, water, toys. She did what she had to
do to get along in the new setting, but her heart remained
sealed. She sat on her teacher's lap and let herself be hugged
but did not hug back.

Sixteen days later Helen was changed. Two brief weeks
after leaving the cottage, her fingers began to talk nonstop,

and her hugs and kisses flowed without effort in the wake of an unbearable joy. The joy of finding . . . and of being found.

~

BECAUSE WE KNOW the story, we know what happened to bring about this transformation. It was the moment at the well house. The miracle flash of inner comprehension finally came as Helen and her teacher filled a mug at the pump. Helen felt the frigid water splashing over her hand . . . then the hand of her teacher giving her its name, signing the word "water." Helen again felt the water . . . again, the word . . . and then . . . it happened. With an almost military stillness, Helen's attention began scavenging deep in the clouded corridors of the past. Submerged there, like treasure in the wreck of a ship, were the few simple words she had heard as a toddler just before silence flooded in. In that single moment of exquisite inner connection, an old, weary heart broke free from more than five years of inner isolation and became a child once more. Called to the bars of her cage yet again, *this* time she felt it swing open. Widely. Fantastically. Open.

~

GOD HONORED ANNE Sullivan's courage and did for the mind of her student what He does for the hearts of His children. He set her free. He gave her a moment of meeting that brought her back into communication with the outside world. Her parents, who had been told more than once through the years that their daughter was an idiot and incapable of being taught, watched as Helen grew and changed. By the age of ten, she was corresponding with European friends — in French. At seventeen, she not only passed every subject on the Harvard entrance exam, she also did it with honors in English and German — receiving the highest score in English of any other candidate for Harvard or Radcliff. It was in *English* —

the place of her former devastation—that Helen found her place of ultimate triumph.

> Suddenly, I understood. Caught up in the first joy I had known since my illness, I reached out eagerly to Annie's ever-ready hand, begging for new words to identify whatever objects I touched. Spark after spark of meaning flew from hand to hand and, miraculously, affection was born. From the well-house there walked two enraptured beings calling each other "Helen" and "Teacher."[2]

Though they had been together constantly for over a month by this time, sharing everything, this, in a sense, is the day Helen Keller and her beloved Anne Sullivan truly "met."

"Spark after spark of meaning flew from hand to hand and miraculously, affection was born." These words, written by Helen a full sixty years later, summarize the essence of what I mean when I use the term "moment of meeting."

When God sets us free through a meeting with Jesus, affection is born. Who can say how or why? It's not as if, in these moments with Him, God hides His honesty and just says easy, cheerful things. He didn't with me. Sometimes none of the happy stuff happens, but we still leave dazed by His love for us, overwhelmed by His infinite *goodness* to us! Even when His embrace is an encounter, a confrontation of sin and fear, it is He doing it, and that makes all the difference.

The moment of meeting is a relational event—it is a social encounter with a social God. The Bible tells us how interactive and social God really is. When He creates, He speaks. When He wants us to know what He thought and felt before we were alive, He writes words to us and fills the pages of a book with impassioned declarations. So interactive is He that when, at the end of it all, He wants to do something obviously striking and out of the ordinary, He calls for half an hour of silence in heaven.[3]

This is Who God is. He calls Himself *The Word*. He loves to talk and tell stories. He loves it when we listen. When He comes to us in a moment of meeting, it is not a legal transaction or an educational effort. It is a conversation of the heart.

Not only does the Bible tell us this is true about God; our own lives with God back it up. For instance, there were many things I needed to be taught the day God met with me. I had already been a Christian for fifteen years. I had loved Him and talked with Him, worshiped and obeyed Him for as long as I could remember. Even so, the years of judging God's motives, doubting His goodness, and working to pick up what He seemed to have dropped had taken their toll. They left me with vast, deep areas of my heart that needed His opening touch. I needed The Cottage and the moment of meeting—I needed freedom even after I had walked with God for years. In answer to this need, my Freedom Teacher didn't try to teach me freedom by handing me a list of new and acceptable behaviors— He became my freedom. He didn't just give me information—He embraced me with *transformation*.

The "moment of meeting" is always for the purpose of transformation and, as such, can be called any number of things and occur in any number of ways. When I use the term, I mean a unit of experience, not of time—the moment of meeting may not be a moment at all. It could be a year of slow, repeated encounters that gradually but completely turn the heart to a new awareness of Him.

～

HOWEVER IT COMES, it is God who orchestrates this moment in fulfillment of His own promise in Jeremiah 31:33: "This is the covenant which I will make with [them] . . . I will put My law within them, and on their heart I will write it; and I will be their God, and they shall be My people." The writer of Hebrews quotes this same passage to signify what Jesus accomplished by inaugurating the new covenant in His own blood.[4] The New Testament repeats this in 2 Corinthians by telling us that God's law is transferred from "tablets of stone" to "tablets of human hearts" (3:3). God Himself writes again with His finger as He did in days past, but this time not on stone. This time He writes with the finger of His Spirit on the very muscle of love itself, the strong storehouse of passionate affection that is the human heart.

In the personal fulfillment of this Scripture, every Christian is pursued by God in very clear and life-changing ways. How He does this pursuing is often hidden from us, and it's usually not until much later that we begin to see the divine timing and planning that went into our encounter with Him.

God will never coerce or force the second reach from one of His children. He doesn't make us respond with affection to Him. I believe that to accomplish His goal of freeing us for a genuine response to Him, God often lets a situation arise that only a joyous, loving God would allow: He sets up a moment of meeting that arrests us with His grace and goodness. He sets up the divine surprise of our lives.

Just because our God won't force a response of affection from us doesn't mean He won't do everything possible to get the conditions right for allowing it to happen. Every Christian, I believe, eventually ends up caught in the crosshairs of His desire for a moment of personal meeting. There really is a wilder, happily crafty side of God that is creative in its wooing. He plans a moment of jarring awareness, a meeting with Himself from which it is almost impossible for the human heart to walk away. To this, countless humbled Christians can testify.

Jesus is good at this. He's an expert at letting us think we're in control of our lives—all the while quietly, tenderly arranging to turn our arrogance into something useful to Him. His own disciples, for instance, thought they had everything figured out—at least to the point where, on the night before He died, they felt the time was right for an argument about who would sit next to Him when He became king of Israel. Like a bunch of kids fighting for the front seat in a Volkswagen sailing over the Grand Canyon, I can picture Jesus listening in, then mildly suggesting they might *all* want to buckle up.

No shame-based lectures about behaving like real disciples, no sermons about selfishness and pride, just the good old bone-jarring, gut-wrenching surprise of God. Whatever the disciples' immediate expectations were of that Passover weekend, clearly they did not dream big enough. They wanted Him to stay and be king for a while—they would help Him rule. He wanted them to be kings and rule with Him for eternity.

THE MOMENT OF meeting is something that can never be humanly orchestrated or imitated. It's strange to realize that most Christian behavior can be replicated. In fact, in his book *Disappointment with God,* Philip Yancey talks about how most of it has been—by him, during his days as a religious skeptic attending a Christian college. And, it's true—the local Moose Lodge has as many nice, caring, generous people as a typical church can claim. So, what's the difference? If helping people is the primary reason for existence on this earth, why does it matter if you're a church or the Volunteer Fireman's Charity Bazaar?

Yancey relates the story of his family that shows us in earthly terms a glimpse of the answer to this question. One time on a visit to his mother—who had been widowed years earlier, in the month of Philip's first birthday—they spent the afternoon together looking through a box of old photos. A certain picture of him as an eight-month-old baby caught his eye. Tattered and bent, it looked too banged up to be worth keeping, so he asked her why, with so many other better pictures of him at the same age, she had kept this one. Yancey writes, "My mother explained to me that she had kept the photo as a memento, because during my father's illness it had been fastened to his iron lung."[5]

During the last four months of his life, Yancey's father lay on his back, completely paralyzed by polio at the age of twenty-four, encased from the neck down in a huge, cylindrical breathing unit. With his two young sons banned from the hospital due to the severity of his illness, he had asked his wife for pictures of her and their two boys. Because he was unable to move even his head, the photos had to be jammed between metal knobs so that they hung within view above him—the only thing he could see. The last four months of his life were spent looking at the faces he loved.

"I have often thought of that crumpled photo, for it is one of the few links connecting me to the stranger who was my father," Yancey writes.

> Someone I have no memory of, no sensory knowledge
> of, spent all day, every day thinking of me, devoting
> himself to me, loving me. . . . The emotions I felt
> when my mother showed me the crumpled photo
> were the very same emotions I felt that February
> night in a college dorm room when I first believed in
> a God of love. *Someone is there, I realized.* Someone is
> there who loves me. It was a startling feeling of wild

hope, a feeling so new and overwhelming that it
seemed fully worth risking my life on.[6]

THIS MEETING WITH His child is a time over which God hov-
ers protectively. He orchestrates this moment, sometimes for
years, because He intends for each of us to have something so
sacred, so much our own with Him that we realize the truth of
what He has been saying all along. He doesn't want just well-
behaved converts; He wants *children*. He doesn't want us just
doing credit to His image; He wants His image to have
entrance into the deepest part of our inner world. He wants the
guts of us to get mixed up with His grace.

I know this is what God wanted for me all those years ago.
He could see how trapped I was. He wanted a free heart that
obeyed out of love and relationship, not out of fear and the
dread of consequences. Ultimately, He wanted my free heart
to return freely to Him. Just as Lincoln gave the slave girl a
choice, God wanted me to have more than freedom *from* something; He wanted me to put my freedom *toward* something —
toward relationship with Him. So, using The Cottage to
prepare my heart, God set me up for a moment of meeting
with Him that has become bedrock in my soul.

BECAUSE THE MOMENT of meeting is extraordinarily personal,
it will never be captured anywhere but in the two hearts in
which it happens. Like the fly ball you caught with your dad at
the World Series, it can be talked about with friends and
described in vivid detail. The ball can even be viewed by others as it sits on the mantle under glass. But the real event, when
you both knew you were going to catch the ball even before it
came whizzing, arcing down at you and slammed into the
pocket of your new birthday mitt — that moment when he

held your shaking seven-year-old hands steady within his own—will always belong to the two of you. There is a No Trespassing sign over this lightning strike of the Father God's love in your life because it was put together by Him to say something important and special to *you*. Just you.

There are so many things we can give to each other in the church. But not this. We can help search for truth, study Scripture, find answers, and pray. We can enter into worship together and accompany each other through crisis, but no human has the code that activates the sudden flash of inner knowing, the divine ripping away of darkness that leaves the soul undone by what the spirit sees.

Only God could come to Job and leave him repentant and happily humbled just by showing up for a talk. Job's friends had been talking for weeks with only agitation to show for it. This is how it works with Jesus. He insists on coming to us personally and showing Himself for who He is. Our best efforts cannot abbreviate the time involved or preprogram the place. All we can do is wait. Like helpless midwives, we can only watch and pray and wait as someone we care about, some questing friend, finds himself lovingly birthed into new freedom by God.

I remember spending many months talking to a man at the place where I worked about the reality of God. Though he was a confirmed agnostic, this seemed to be his favorite topic. So, over and over we discussed the reasons I believed in Jesus. I recommended he read and study the Bible; I gave him Josh McDowell's classic *Evidence That Demands a Verdict;* I prayed for him, loaned him books from our home library, and did my best to make it all make sense.

After many months, however, in a conversation one day he reviewed some of what we'd gone over, handed back the latest book, cocked his head to one side and said matter-of-factly, "You know, Vicki, I still don't see how you can be so sure God exists."

Boy, that ripped it! What was this guy—*blind?* "Look," I said in my okay-buster-now-you've-asked-for-it voice that my kids really love, "here's the deal. I know He's real because I've *met* Him. Okay? I've *met* Him. That's it. I can't prove Him to you but He's as real to me as you are because I've met Him and if you really want to know, for *me* that's the bottom line. That's why *this* little Christian cookie believes!" (or words to that effect). I'm sure he was helped right along into the arms of God by my sweet, secure manner. He's probably on some gentle therapist's couch even now.

However that may be, I know that for me it was a clarifying experience. In my exasperation with this guy and his quest, I had to admit my even greater exasperation with Christ. Why purposely call all of mankind to Himself (billions of us) then make it such an agonizing one-on-one journey? Why send His people out with a message that is *purposely* not transferable— designed *not* to be neatly exportable. With all that's at stake for everyone involved, why not go for efficiency, productivity? Why not give us a neatly packaged 3.5 floppy of neuron-friendly software for the serious questor's brain? Better yet, why not something tasty that could be mixed with hot milk at bedtime and—presto!—wake up worshiping?!

Because. For God the moment of meeting is still the heartbeat of His heaven. It is sheer, unencumbered communion, and for Him it is important enough that He took His own Triune Communion to the cross. This is the God of covenant oneness, deep fellowship, fierce fidelity, and celebratory love. Communion—oneness—fellowship, this is the only air heaven has. It's the only food fit for eating at His table.

That's how it is with this amazing, infinite, tenaciously interactive God. *I love how He loves us!* He is so cheerfully ready for a ruckus, so supremely prepared for our resistance as He works to free us. Even for those who have walked with Him all their lives, He is the God who hunts for the hearts of His children—eager for the moment of finding . . . eager to be found.

Face it. It's true. Even with all the cozier, more controllable gods around us, you and I—we Christians—have somehow managed to choose the most difficult and demanding of all gods. Difficult because ultimately He won't settle for less than He deserves. He won't applaud external displays of obedience and affection that are just hollow acts of compliance. Demanding because He wants the most expensive relationship there is—something that couldn't be bought with anything less than blood. What He wants—*what He deserves*—are sons and daughters who approach Him, knowing how much He is worth and therefore how much they are loved.

God loves to engage our heart and surprise our mind. He loves to give each of us our own story with Him. Our stories are, in a very real way, our truest, most hope-inducing gift to another person. Besides, that's where we all seem to end up— back at that cherished moment with God when we met Him. Really *met* Him. So I'm always greatly entertained when Christians tell me they don't believe in experiences. "Can't be trusted," they say, "too emotional—not safe."

Safe? Who said anything about safe? This is the God who sneaks around corners, drops out of trees, spends years letting you ruin His reputation, all the while setting you up for the moment of inner ambush that unmasks you to yourself and frees you for Him. If *that's* not emotional, what is?!

He's the master of this sacred sting of utter undoing. So much so that it remains the one story we never tire of telling.

Our story. The story of the day *God* showed up and in His hand was our photo, all mangled and stained with blood from the place above Him where it hung. He came to find *us,* and all the tinder, all the fellowship-fire hopes we'd been quietly stockpiling in our hearts for so many years, ignited in a single moment of meeting.

Fourteen

THE SECOND REACH

The same God who allows fear to drive us to Him for rescue calls us to abandon that fear as we begin to minister to Him. This is the pattern. Though our salvation may have initially had more to do with avoiding hell, God draws us to a place where our preoccupation is almost exclusively with heaven. That's the second reach of our heart toward Him. Though we may have been brought to a place of new communion with Him through The Cottage, we find ourselves wanting to approach God for no other reason than to bless Him. This reach of our heart is never compulsory. It is entirely ours to control, but if given, it has a powerful impact upon His heart.

IN CHAPTER 12 I told of my experience at the age of nine while in Ecuador that set up the "prison" from which the Lord had to release me. In seeking to identify the substructure of the cell that imprisoned me for so many years, I have found this one simple, seemingly innocent question: "Are you sure your God is good?"

During the moment I stood in front of so many starving mothers and children, this question seemed distant, almost annoying. Mixed up in the immediate emotional turmoil, it hardly seemed worth considering. I didn't realize it then, but I was following in ancient female footsteps, being lied to by an ancient, enemy tongue.

In the years that followed, the lie became relentless and I felt troubled, often anxious. I was committed unhesitatingly to the truth of the Bible. Its claims about God were real, I told myself. He is the one true, living, good, righteous, loving God. He is omniscient, omnipresent, and omnipotent—these were words whose meanings I knew. Because the implications of these truths were clear, even the apparent need to consider a question concerning the goodness of God troubled me. The God I believed in was *obviously* good, clearly superior to anyone, anywhere.

This was the conviction of my young heart, yet what my eyes had seen kept flashing a clear, conflicting message. Like a slice of subliminal advertising, the hits came subtly—persistently. Over and over, the images of bowls and babies infiltrated the normal routine of my life in the suburbs.

The few minutes on that busy street corner in Guayaquil became a turning point in my life. They shaped me. Not completely, of course, but significantly. It seemed as though two trains heading toward each other at the same speed, sharing the same track, were converging. The reality of the human suffering was undeniable. It was documentable and factually evident. The reality of my convictions about God was also documentable (scripturally) and *faith*-fully evident. These two indisputable truths presented themselves to me. Both sets of facts seemed undeniable as they converged at the street corner covered with mothers and children. Within moments that day, I was in the middle of a train wreck. Like a boxcar pile-up, two sets of logical assumptions that gave structure, power, and reality to the two trains came together in a conflagration.

If God is all-powerful, all-knowing, and all-good, why

would He allow what is obviously so wrong, painful, and unfair? Surely, if His "eye is on the sparrow," then He can't have missed this scene. Surely if He is all-powerful, He could change it if He wanted to, and—if He is truly good—He would want to. This much was simple enough. Therefore, because He had not changed these children's lot in life (or the many millions like them the world over) one of my convictions about His attributes had to be incorrect. Which one was it? Satan helped me here: "Are you sure this God is a *good* God?" he asked.

Don't imagine this to be an advanced thought process for a nine-year-old. Our homes are filled with these amazing, tiny philosophers who are morally astute and innately sensitive to the nature of the sovereign God. (I had some of my deepest conversations with our boys when they were between the ages of four and six.) If, as I was, children are exposed to scriptural truth early in their lives, they can compute two plus two ethically long before they can do it on paper as a math equation. This is a good thing, but it also sets the stage for train wrecks because, as happened with me, I did not think to discuss the struggle openly with anyone.

IN THE PREVIOUS chapters, you've read brief bits of how this situation affected my life and how God took me to freedom. My prison wasn't so much a place I couldn't leave. It was a prison because I didn't have anywhere else to go. Something like a hobo who lives in an old boxcar because he's avoiding what normal society requires, I stayed at the site of the wreck and made myself a home.

I sifted though all the debris, finding something useful in every piece of scrap metal. Over a period of years, I built what I thought was a pretty creative, Swiss Family Robinson kind of

Christian life. I never got rid of the aftermath of the collision, and I never cleared away any of the issues that were troubling me about God. I just lived with them. I did this because it was easier than making a decision to trust God in this area of human suffering.

I ruminated on human-pain-vs.-the-goodness-of-God issues constantly, in every conceivable setting, and came up with the same answer every time. I was safer here in this box-car city. So, I never went near any clear-cut decisions to trust God again in the area of human suffering.

Because I trusted Him in many other areas of life instead—where to work, who to date, where to go to college—I felt content and close to Him. As long as I stayed among the rusty remains in that one area of life, sifting, sorting, finding a use for everything, doing helpful, creative things for others, I felt strong. Too strong.

Even for someone living in these grim conditions, my Cottage experience was tough. It didn't seem safe or comfortable—probably because, by any normal rule of measurement, it was both. By the time I got there, I felt such strong survivor's guilt that owning anything nice (that wasn't also useful and shareable) became a source of guilt and fear. So God saw to it that I was very nicely provided for. My Cottage had none of the hallmarks of some others I've heard of. It didn't cut me off from Christian fellowship—I had good friendships, a caring family, challenging teachers. I was financially secure and physically healthy. I wasn't being rejected socially. In fact, it was during this time that I got engaged. Even my fiancé was not a problem—a loving, Christian, Harvard grad with a fun, robust personality. Still, I sensed he didn't have what it took for life in a boxcar, so we broke up. All in all, my life was more than fine by anyone's standards but my own. It still remains for me the coldest, darkest, most spiritually and emotionally difficult time of my life.

Freedom came, as I related in chapter 1, suddenly and absolutely. Though I have had several refresher visits to The Cottage since then, my first moment of meeting was profoundly transforming. Overnight, bulldozers, earthmoving equipment, and builders had prepared for me a new place to live—a new, *living* home in a grove of giant, spring-fed willows. Spiritually speaking, I was more than free; I was alive in Christ in ways I had never experienced before. I wasn't afraid of God anymore—I *knew* He was good. Absolutely, undeniably, irreversibly good—good in the face of human pain.

I can't tell you exactly what changed in me that day, but I am still radically different because of what He did in my heart.

"THE SECOND REACH" is a metaphorical term I used in earlier chapters that describes the change in motivation that took place in Helen Keller's heart after she found her freedom. She began to do things for reasons far beyond her desire to survive.

This is similar to the change in attitude and motivation that takes place in our hearts after we have been set free by God. Just as our response of affection and gratitude toward God is very much like Helen's after she had her moment of meeting at the pump, I think of the second reach as the more intentional, premeditated response we give to God over and over for the rest of our lives. The second reach, therefore, is not an event by which we experience God, but an attitude with which we approach Him. It is centered upon Him, not ourselves and, as such, it is the arena within which our ministry to Him takes place.

It has been in the aftermath of finding my freedom that I've offered my deepest ministry to God. That is because it is in the very place of my wounding that He chose to live and engage me in communion. And now it is from this place of communion that I minister to His heart. Together we have constructed a sanctuary on the ashes of my former sin and shame, and now my old wound serves as the site of my new priesthood: ministering to His heart for the simple purpose of bringing Him joy.

~

I HOPE THE freedom and simplicity of what I'm sharing here is apparent. The operative question we ask as we prepare to minister to God is: Of what is God worthy? Given Who He is, what does He deserve? There's nothing very complicated in what I do or say when I'm ministering to God, but these questions help clarify the shift of focus that is necessary as we lift our hearts to Him.

To show you how God has, slowly, over many years, brought me to a place of ministering to Him in the arena of human suffering, I want to tell of a day four years ago that was pivotal in this process. I was asked to lead a conference about ministering to God. Because the last day of the conference was a Sunday, members of this church decided to spend twelve hours ministering to God one by one in the corporate setting. This allowed the larger congregation to enter into a place of agreement with whomever was talking to God and to support each other as we opened our hearts and presented our gifts. The emphasis of such a day is centered on God Himself, not on the people present.

So we agreed ahead of time that after the normal church service, the ministry to God would begin with a shift in focus. I encouraged people not to assess everything for its value to them personally or to someone who needed salvation. This required that we would all put a guard on our minds and agree not to indulge in questions that implied the kind of entitlement to which we have become accustomed in the church (that is, Am I feeling blessed, taught, "fed," ministered to, . . . ?). Instead we agreed to enter into a place of priestly jealousy to bless God alone. We also agreed not to look for any kind of response from God as indication that He was aware of our effort. In an act of confidence in His promise to be present with us, we set about the happy task of blessing Him—with no strings attached.

It was a remarkable day and we witnessed many beautiful expressions of ministry. Always facing away from the congregation and toward the front of the church, whoever had the microphone would talk to God with the rest of us as backup ministers. Some sang solos, some brought banners that had been in the making for months. One proud and grateful father presented his children to God—each with a bouquet of flowers that were laid on the steps at the front of the sanctuary. Young men played their guitars, drums, or trumpets; a mother and daughter did an interpretive dance to a recorded worship song; poetry was read; artwork was presented; marriages were consecrated; and a young seminary student came—books in tow—to read to God his favorite portion of an essay about grace. While the adults were taking turns with the mike, the children were in the back of the church, working quietly at low tables, drawing things "for God" and occasionally trundling up to put them on the steps.

At the end of the twelve hours, the day was brought to a close with prayer. Even at the end, several people were still waiting to bring God their gifts of personal ministry and worship. The pastor seemed amazed and delighted by his congregation's response to God.

It was in this setting that I ministered something to God that may have some significance for you as a reader of this book, now that you are familiar with my story. What I brought to God that day was a copy of an article from *Guideposts* magazine. In it was the story of Kim Phuc—the young, napalm-covered girl who had been photographed on June 8, 1972. Only nine years old, she was shown running terrified and naked from the bombs that had already covered her body with savage burns. Throughout the West, this photo became a symbol of the horror of the Vietnam War. When this incident occurred, I was nineteen—a full decade from my time in Ecuador, and just a year before I was to visit The Cottage. The event was one more reminder of my ongoing struggle.

When I first saw the *Guideposts* article, my heart began to race. It had been many years since I had found my freedom. Nevertheless, emotions from the early seventies came flooding back. As I read the article, I discovered that Kim Phuc, whom I had always assumed to be dead, had survived. In fact, she had more than survived. She had become a Christian, married, settled in Canada, and had a child. The article highlighted her meeting and reconciliation with the U.S. commander who had ordered the bombing that had maimed her. In the intervening years he, too, had become a Christian and subsequently, a military chaplain. At their meeting, they wept and hugged, not just in reconciliation but also in celebration of their new status as brother and sister in a kingdom that would be forever ruled by the Prince of Peace. They have since ministered together, speaking of God's goodness and leading many in the path of forgiveness.

As I read that article, I felt the enormity of my error. For years I had assumed the worst, but God had been quietly, incredibly working out the best. I was silent before Him. During my years of struggle, I had felt justified in judging this God based on what my eyes had seen. What about what my eyes had *not* yet seen? What of all the miraculous endings to stories of human suffering that I will never know—until I meet the people in these stories in heaven and rejoice with them over the goodness of our amazing God.

So it was that some time later in the church in Canada, I brought the article to God with a broken and contrite heart. I spoke to Him about how infinitely worthy He is of my trust in every situation. I used the article as a symbol of His unwavering, though often hidden, goodness—His ability to bring even the most horrific of life's experiences into a place of healing grace. I repented of my judgments, my many judgments against Him, and vowed a new and real trust. I ended my words to Him that day with a statement that went something like this: "I declare that You, Lord, are worthy of my complete confidence regardless of what I think I know. You are *always* to be trusted—regardless of the human reality before me. I say to You that You are infinite; I am not. I do not know the end of the story of humanity's suffering—but *You know.* And trusting You—giving to you the absolute, unquestioning allegiance of which You are so worthy—is more than my duty; it is my privilege. It will be an honor to trust You here and now—before I know the end of things, while faith is still necessary to find Your face."

IN THE REMAINDER of this chapter, I will share some examples of how ministry to God can take place verbally, in any number of different daily situations. This is what ministry to God *can* look like, not necessarily what it *should* look like.

EVANGELISM

When we minister to God through evangelism, our mindset shifts from "Here's what Jesus will do for you if you accept Him as your Savior" (that is, rescue you from hell, carry you to heaven, free you from drugs, give you a wonderful plan for your life . . .) to this question: Of what is God worthy? Answer: God is worthy of every person's absolute allegiance. Indeed, the day will come when every knee will bow.[1] The mindset of ministering to God through evangelism therefore is:

First, minister to God: "Lord, I ask you to give to Yourself the life of my friend Sue. I know, Father, that you will not override anyone's will, but I also know how creative and convincing you were with me. I've seen you make Yourself real to people who had no interest in you. Would you do that now for Sue? You deserve her life, Lord. You are worthy of her utmost commitment. You have created her for Yourself, Father, and her heart, her praise rightly belong to You. Give Yourself the gift of Sue, please, Lord, for Your name's sake and for the glory of Your kingdom."

Then minister to the person: "Sue, have you ever sensed that you've been created for more than just the daily grind —that you have a purpose? Have you ever felt that there may be someone noble enough to deserve your ultimate allegiance? Do you ever hear a voice deep within telling you that you're worth more than this? Can I tell you what you are worth, Sue? Can I tell you what God has already said about how important you are to Him—what you mean to Him?

MARRIAGE

When we minister to God through marriage, we move from questions like "What will give us a successful marriage? How can we as a couple be happier and more fulfilled? How can we divorce-proof our home?" to "What is God's due in this relationship? Of what attitudes and actions is He worthy? Who are we, as a couple, to God? What image of His own Oneness does God deserve to see lived out here on earth through our marriage?"

First, minister to God: "Lord Jesus Christ, our marriage does not belong to us; it belongs to You. Please begin to satisfy Your own heart in our union. Give Yourself, through our daily reactions to each other, a clear view of You and Your bride, the church. Let our lives 'speak' to You about the nature of Your own Oneness, by the daily choices we make toward fidelity."

Then minister to each other: "David, I know you belong first to God and then to me. Because of that, I want to repent to you for thinking I own your time, your energy, and your attention. I want to release you from the 'you owe me' attitude that I have carried toward you. I confess that it is not your job to keep me happy. I belong to God. He is my source and He deserves my absolute trust on issues of protection and in the area of expectations. I am also asking God to help me know how to understand you and how to meet your needs before you have to ask. I commit myself to respond first to Him and then to you in all the areas of our life together. I want to respond to His assessment of you, not to what I think I'm seeing. God is your judge; as your wife I relinquish that back to Him. I will respond to you out of my fellowship and oneness with Him, not out of fear of your rejection or disappointment in me. I want to support you in prayer to be the kind of man of which our God is worthy. I am committing to pray for you regularly. I'm going to ask God to put a hunger in you for the attributes that His own nobility deserves in a man who bears His name."

"Doris, I know that you belong to God first and then to me. Because of that I want to release you from the demands I tend to make for my needs to be met. I want to free you to a place of priesthood to God where you can respond to Him first and to me second. Because I want Him to have what He deserves from us as a couple, I am going to trust Him to show you how to meet my needs. I commit myself to doing the same with you. I agree to respond first to God Himself and not to you, your tone of voice, your moods, your demands. I want to know you on a level that allows me to pursue your heart and know you as a friend. You may have to help me from time to time, but I agree to work toward a knowledge of you (through an awareness heightened by God) that will show me how to meet your emotional needs. I will not use a 'do list' that I can work through and be done with my responsibility. No more lists. God deserves that, as a husband, I approach you as He does His church—through relationship born of intimate knowledge and steadfast love. Therefore, this is in my heart to do."

ISSUES OF TEENAGE CHASTITY

Discussion with teenagers about sex shifts from a precautionary "Don't have sex before marriage because you could get a sexually transmitted disease or get pregnant" message to "Don't have sex before marriage because it is ultimately an act of infidelity, and infidelity is a form of breaking covenant with God."

First, minister to God: "Father, I acknowledge that Robert is Your son before he is our son and that Emma is Your daughter before she is ours. You deserve to have the first response of their young hearts. We as their parents do not deserve this, neither do their girlfriend and boyfriend, nor do their teachers. You alone are worthy of their first and full allegiance. Jesus, please teach them about the Father's heart. Teach them Your own willingness to walk in sexual purity because of Your love for Your Father. Give them a glimpse of the enormity of their own worth to You by virtue of Your sacrifice. Give our children — these incredible living treasures — an understanding of who they are to You. Please show them how You feel about Your Son so they will understand how much they mean to You. Also, Holy Spirit, please be strong in our children. Let them hear Your voice saying, 'This is the way, walk in it.' Guide their paths, protect their hearts and minds, because You, God, are worthy of their highest commitment. Their covenant with You deserves their absolute fidelity."

Then minister to the teens: "Robert and Emma, we hereby consecrate your lives to God's pleasure. As your parents, we say to you that you belong first and foremost to Him. You exist because He gave you life and He deserves your full praise. Only He is worthy of your worship. As members of His priesthood, we are more committed to *His* pleasure than to yours. You need to know that you and your health are not more important to us than God. The primary issue for us is not whether you will get a sexually transmitted disease, but whether you will break covenant with God. In direct defiance of this age and all that it has told you, we as your parents want you to know that God is worthy of your fidelity. We love and treasure you. We would without hesitation give our lives to save yours. However, your physical lives are not more important than God. You are bound by covenant with Him not just to do His will, but also to engage His heart. Therefore, we commit ourselves to helping you learn ways of ministering to Him with the same caliber of sexual purity and choices toward covenant oneness with God that characterized Jesus when He walked here on earth. His sacrifice for you is your protection. But as your parents, we are jealous for His name to be carried with honor in your lives. Are you willing for us to ask Him to alert you of danger, convict you of sin, and discipline your ways that you may walk righteously before Him?"

CHURCH

Ministering to God through attending church involves a change of attitude. Instead of going to church because we know we will learn about God, see friends, eat donuts, and be blessed, we move to the position that says, "Church is an essential part of my life because it is where I meet with the other members of the priesthood and minister corporately to God's heart."

First, we minister to God: "Lord, this is Your day and I am here in Your presence with Your people for Your pleasure. Father, I am here to meet with You. I come to You as one of many who have been made clean by the blood of Your Son. We are Your royal priesthood, Lord, and as such we come first to minister to You. We are not here just for what we can get from You or to help each other grow. We are here for what we can give to You directly. Show us, Holy Spirit, how to touch Your heart today."

Then we minister to God by actively entering into the worship, prayer, offering, communion, and sermon in whatever way our church celebrates these parts of the service. With each part, we keep our mind stayed on God.

Right now in my own life I am trying to train myself to participate with whomever is "up front" ministering to God. For instance, if someone sings a solo, I position myself before God on behalf of what that person is doing. I picture myself as part of a team effort with the soloist. Though the song is happening in front of me here on earth, I mentally send it "up" to God for His pleasure. I see myself as giving backup and spiritual agreement to what the soloist is doing. I intentionally try not to form opinions about the quality of what's being done or how the person looks. What is happening is first and foremost for God's pleasure and glory, not for my inspection and approval.

It is the expression of a fellow member of the priesthood, and I want to support the gift that person is giving to Him.

Then we minister to people: It is not unusual for God to speak to me during church about the needs of people in the congregation. I could be reminded of a crisis they are facing or be given some insight about how to pray for them, and so forth. Nudged by God, I know that I am not running ahead of Him, trying to handle things on my own, problem-solving for everyone around me. Church is first and foremost for God's pleasure, but God's pleasure is almost always to minister healing and comfort to His people.

Fifteen

THE MINDSET OF
MINISTERING TO GOD

*Is ministering to God a thing of the mind? Yes. We
lead with our heart but it is the mind of Christ in
us that inspires our heart and motivates our behaviors. As we minister to God, we adopt a clear and
certain perspective, an intentional "set" of the mind
toward God.*

*T*HE BATTLE HAD been raging for months. During that
time the fighting had grown so fierce, so deeply divi-
sive, that even family members stood opposite each other on
the battlefield.

"Why are you here?" snarled Ares to his sister. "You tried
to wound me once before—well, now it is my turn!" Raising
his sword, he struck a crushing blow to Athena's head. Her hel-
met, however, was of special metal, and the blow was repelled.

Seething with hatred, Athena struck back. Flinging a huge
boulder, she hit her brother in the neck. He staggered under its
impact and fell. "You silly fool!" she spat derisively. "You want
to fight with me and you don't even know that I am stronger
than you!"

Just then the beautiful Aphrodite ran to Ares' side. Taking
him by the hand, she led him from the battlefield. Further

enraged by this act of intervention, Athena ran after Aphrodite and knocked her down.

"Ha!" she exclaimed as she stood over her battered rivals. "If we immortals had fought, the war would have been over long ago, and Troy would no longer be standing!"[1]

THE ABOVE INTERACTION is not a violent domestic dispute between human beings, but the bloody bickering of three Greek gods warring over the city of Troy. Far from the noble, majestic actions expected of supreme beings, this kind of behavior was common among the deities that the Greeks and Romans worshiped.

The gods of these ancient empires were famous for their petty rivalries and moral indiscretions. Mythology is filled with accounts of their jealous rages, adulterous liaisons, schemes to injure and discredit each other, and elaborate plots of revenge for slights suffered. All in all, these gods, though empowered with various supernatural attributes, were more human than godlike in character and temperament.

In like manner, ancient Babylonian gods had basic physical needs that mirrored the human frailty of those who served them. Every day, priests would bathe, clothe, and feed the idols they worshiped. The Babylonians believed that the essence of any god they served lived inside their carved image of it. An idol was not just an earthly representation of a higher, heavenly being, but the actual body of a god.

Because of this, great care was given to the image itself, and no detail was overlooked in providing for its comfort and upkeep. Several times each day, trays of food and flowers were brought to its chamber; holy water was sprinkled to purify its surroundings; and curtains were drawn to protect its privacy while eating.

Other cultures of the time worried about the health and strength of their gods. For instance, many sun-worshiping, agrarian societies would watch with concern the apparent waning of their god's energies during the winter solstice. Pale and weak after the blazing work of summer, the winter sun gave anemic, shallow warmth. Ultimately, it seemed clear to the concerned worshipers that their god was either sick or dying.

Anxious to restore the sun's failing energy in time for the upcoming season of fertility and growth, they would ceremonially kill a strong, virile young man or fertile young woman and offer the blood to the sun god to drink. In this way it was thought that the sun's strength was replenished and future crops were secured. By drawing new life from humanity, the god's vitality—at least for the coming summer—was assured.

IN THESE EXAMPLES, we see a pattern. Throughout history, people have often worshiped gods whose temperaments, passions, and shortcomings were as human as their own. There has been a tendency to project upon the objects of our worship what is most real for us.

This pattern was shattered by the God of ancient Israel. The dynamic of a god's similarity to, and dependence upon, the people it governed was thoroughly dismantled by the God of the Hebrews. Yahweh, also the God of the present-day Christian church, came to be known to His people as the everywhere-present, all-knowing, all-powerful One who is complete in Himself.

In stark contrast to the gods of other nations, there is no record of Yahweh waiting patiently on His pedestal for His bath. There is no account of Him anticipating with hungry helplessness the arrival of His next meal or borrowing enough energy to survive an approaching summer.

Instead Israel was subject to a much different interaction with her God than that experienced by any of her neighbors. As worshipers of an invisible God, Israel was not allowed (nor actually able) to define in any chiseled, visible way His shape and substance. As the follower of One who moves about at will, she was allowed no stationary stone image by which to monitor His movements. Yahweh was utterly "other" and His people understood this. In fact, whenever Israel lapsed in this understanding and approached Yahweh as other nations approached their gods, He would throw off her efforts with disgust:

"Hear, O my people, and I will speak,
O Israel, and I will testify against you:
I am God, your God. . . .
I have no need of a bull from your stall
or of goats from your pens,
for every animal of the forest is mine,
and the cattle on a thousand hills.
I know every bird in the mountains,
and the creatures of the field are mine.
If I were hungry I would not tell you,
for the world is mine, and all that is in it.
Do I eat the flesh of bulls
or drink the blood of goats?"
(Psalm 50:7,9-13, NIV, emphasis mine)

To whom will you compare me?
Or who is my equal?" says the Holy One. . . .
Do you not know?
Have you not heard?
The LORD is the everlasting God,
The Creator of the ends of the earth.

He will not grow tired or weary,
and his understanding no one can fathom.

He gives strength to the weary
and increases *the power of the weak.*
Even youths grow tired and weary,
and young *men stumble and fall;*
But those who hope in the LORD
will renew *their strength.*
They will soar on wings like eagles;
they will run and not grow weary,
they will walk and not be faint.
(Isaiah 40:25,28-31, NIV, emphasis mine)

In these passages God sets Himself apart from the gods of Israel's neighbors. Though surrounded by societies whose deities required constant upkeep, Israel's God was not weak and dependent, but mighty and strong. In His personal care for His creation, He was the God who "knows every bird of the heavens." "Every animal of the forest" belonged to Him. His knowledge was "beyond scrutiny."

When we Christians try to minister to this same God, we should not imagine that we can meet His needs, for He doesn't have any. Neither should we, like the Babylonians, try to minister to Him in a way that reflects our nature instead of His.

This can be an area of struggle for many of us. It's not unusual for me, like worshipers of long ago, to see God through the filter of my own finite nature. Unless clearly focused on Him as He is presented in the Bible, I tend to view God through the lens of my human frailty. In many subtle ways, I superimpose upon God what is true for me and then, because of who *I* am, I have trouble trusting Him. I transfer to

God's account my own failing resources, then worry that I will "use up" His love or deplete His provision. Instead of trusting His welcome and approaching Him boldly, I inch forward cautiously, with uneasy, tentative steps. My own narrowness of soul hides the breadth of His heart, and I fear causing Him just enough trouble to outdistance His grace. In short, if I don't trust what the Scriptures tell me about God, I expect to find God as fragile in His faithfulness as I am and as ready to cut off communication as His comfort might require.

Over the years, however, I've found this to be a false set of fears. It is not an idol that I worship, but the living God! It is not a brittle, breakable stone image, but the living Rock—the Rock of Ages—who is my refuge! Time and again, God has shown me that it is not my own nature but the nature of His Son Jesus, the precious Cornerstone,[2] upon whose substance is built my ministry to Him.

Jesus, our marvelous High Priest, can "sympathize with our weaknesses," but cannot be defined by them. He "who has been tempted in all things as we are, yet without sin" (Hebrews 4:15) has redeemed me. Far from revitalizing Him with the gift of my life, I have become the beneficiary of His.[3]

Now I, in communion with millions of fellow followers of Jesus Christ, drink *His* blood, eat *His* flesh, and draw from Him the strength to embrace, not just another summer—but eternity! So it is that we Christians take our life from God, never He from us. We draw our strength from the vast reservoir of His supply, and from this supply we too become strong.

Through the blood of Jesus we have become the sons of God, and from the security of this relationship we begin to respond to God with confidence. Our heavenly Father has genetically reproduced in us all that is necessary for ministry to Him. He has, through the person of His Son Jesus, given to us the very essence of His own nature, filled us with the Holy Spirit, and infused us with the mind of Christ.

FOR JESUS IT is unthinkable that He would ever live apart from constant communion with His Father and the Holy Spirit. We know this because everything Jesus did on earth was sovereignly synchronized with The Music of His Father's will.[4] Every move He made was dependent upon the leading of the Holy Spirit. This is one of the mysteries of the Incarnation. Jesus, God the Son, brought the communion of the Godhead with Him when He came. In His life on this earth, every choice He made was consistent with the heavenly Oneness He had always shared. Though curtailed by human flesh and all its limitations, Jesus still operated in complete fellowship and oneness with the other two members of the Godhead. He had to trust His Father's voice more than the human voices around Him. He had to trust the leading of the Holy Spirit more than the road in front of Him.

Because this daily faith-walk of Christ was real, we know His temptation was real as well. Perhaps it was in the midst of His wilderness temptation that Jesus made His most significant choices toward oneness. Matthew 4 tells us, "Then Jesus was led up by the Spirit into the wilderness to be tempted by the devil. And after He had fasted forty days and forty nights, He then became hungry. And the tempter came and said to Him, 'If You are the Son of God, command that these stones become bread'" (verses 1-3, NASB).

It was, I believe, clear that all Diabolos (the scriptural Greek name for the Devil) had to do was lead the hungry Jesus to abdicate His state of dependence upon the Holy Spirit, withdraw His trust in the Father, and provide food for Himself in order for the redemptive plan of God to fail.

The only way Jesus could have made food for Himself was to do it alone, separate from His Father's will and the Spirit's empowering, separate from the communion of the Godhead. For Jesus to tell stones to become bread (a seemingly harmless suggestion) He would have had to declare a separated survival from His Father and the Spirit and reclaim His divine power.

This Jesus could certainly do. Jesus knew who He was. He had just come from His baptism, where He had heard God's voice declare Him to be His very own "beloved Son." As the Son of God, Jesus knew He had the power to provide anything He needed. Furthermore, He had ample motivation. After more than a month of wandering in the sun-scorched wasteland without food, Jesus' body wanted food. Matthew 4:2 tells us, "He then became hungry." I believe He felt death tugging at Him and His own flesh screaming at Him to provide life for Himself. I think His weakened body could easily have reasoned for its own survival based on all that its incarnated form had come to accomplish. "After all," it could have said, "what good will you be to your Father dead in the desert? How are you going to accomplish His will if you allow yourself to die *this* way, instead of according to the prophetic scriptural texts you've been sent to fulfill? Yes, you came to suffer and die, but not now, not yet. Act! Be true to who you are! You're not weak; you're strong! You're not man; you're God! Act like it! Save yourself . . . for your Father's sake and for the sake of all He has commissioned you to do."

Jesus could have effortlessly made the stone into bread, and that is the crux of this temptation. He could have saved His own life, but not without breaking faith with His Father's will. He would have had to abandon the weakness of His incarnated body, reclaim His sovereign power, and become sufficient for His own need.

Of course, this would have fully satisfied the Devil. Diabolos would have known that all he had to do was draw Jesus, the "second Adam," into taking one independent step. Just one crack in the communion, however innocuous, and the entire messianic mandate would crumble.

The call upon Jesus as He walked on the earth was the same call that is on us as His disciples: to walk in complete union and dependence upon God, wholly entrusting ourselves to His provision. This was the choice set before the weakened Christ: survival separate from His Father's will, or continued dependence with no guarantee of when He would see His need met.

Jesus answered with a clear, succinct declaration of dependence: "It is written, 'Man shall not live on bread alone, but on every word that proceeds out of the mouth of God'" (Matthew 4:4). In choosing this text from the Pentateuch, He sent three clear messages to Diabolos:

1. I am just as fully man as I am God, and I refuse to betray that status by grasping My own provision. Instead, I will find My true food as all men were intended to: in communion with God by feasting on the Word of God.
2. As the second Adam, I am choosing to trust God and His provision regardless of how "good" it may seem to take and eat what has not yet been given to Me.
3. I reject any survival that is not born out of oneness with God.

The final two temptations were different in detail but similar in their agenda.[5] The Enemy's primary goal was to draw Jesus into a place of personal autonomy—separateness from His Father—either by providing for His own physical needs, making independent decisions regarding His mandate, or succumbing to a premature and deathless glory. The Enemy wanted Jesus to strike out on His own and turn His back on the heavenly communion.

Ultimately, the message of Jesus to the Devil was this: I will not, under any circumstance, choose a life separate from My Father. Oneness with Him *is* My life. Unbroken communion with the Father and the Spirit was Christ's continuous choice in the face of every earthly temptation, and so it must be for all of us who wear His name.

IN THE YEARS since my freedom, I have grown in my appreciation of all that Christ accomplished by His choices toward oneness throughout His life on this earth. I have also been convicted about the many times I still opt toward "saving" a situation in my own strength (thereby choosing a separated survival) instead of leaning into the oneness I have been called to share and relying on God's timing and power.

In His desire to help me with this struggle, God has taught me a very simple, practical, and portable process (it seems to work anywhere) for making my everyday decisions from a place of oneness with Him. This has become one of the most profound aspects of the "mind of Christ" available to me, and I want to end the chapter by sharing it with you.

One of the primary ways we can free ourselves for fellowship with God in any situation is by refusing to do anything out of fear. I believe that ungodly fear (the opposite of what the Scriptures speak of as the "fear of God") has ransacked our country. It is the dominant motivator in most personal, corporate, political, and social interactions. This does not mean the *feeling* of fear is always present; it means the *motivational force* of fear is present.

In other words, what propels something forward is dread of possible outcomes. It usually starts with this simple phrase: "What will happen if . . . " and can end with anything from ". . . I don't get to work on time?" to " . . . I don't find the right wife?" Fear is such an accepted and successful motivator that we no longer question its impact on the way we make decisions.

When we were born again into God's kingdom, we became partakers of Jesus Christ, and Jesus never let fear motivate Him. I can't think of a single incident in the Bible when Jesus did something because He was afraid. *Everything* He did (including go to His death on the cross) was an act of fellowship: submitted communion with His Father. All Christians, like Jesus, can choose to do everything out of fellowship with Him and so retain the worship that He is due in each situation.

Some years ago as I was sorting laundry, I felt God speak to my heart one very clear sentence. He said, "Vicki, if it's fear, it's not fellowship, and if it's not fellowship, it's not Me." When I first heard these words in my heart, I knew they were true. I knew the wealth of Scripture supports this understanding, but I gave it no real attention at the time. My days were busy. I was hustling from task to task, and it was two days later when — while vacuuming — I heard the sentence again. This time, however, the words interrupted a concern I was dealing with. One of the couples on the pastoral team of our church seemed to be overwhelmed with life's ongoing crises — sickness, financial setbacks, car problems, and more. In mulling over their situation, I began to plan my time so that I could take them a casserole to show them that we cared. It was at that very moment that I felt the Holy Spirit speak to me the same simple sentence. And then I felt Him say to me this additional thought: "Vicki, there's nothing wrong with taking them a casserole. But there is something wrong with doing it out of fear. I am sufficient for this family and their needs. I will keep them strong. So if you want to take a casserole and celebrate who they are, do that, but don't do it because you're afraid I'm not enough to keep them strong."

Years later, I can still remember the Lord saying that entire paragraph to me in very much those words. This incident has stayed with me because, for the first time, I glimpsed how my fear was betraying me in small, daily ways. Without realizing it, my fear had caused me to act in ways that questioned God's goodness and sufficiency. Because I had never thought of myself as being particularly fearful, I was amazed at the number of times my reason for doing something came out of a dread of the repercussions if it didn't get done. Or I feared what someone else might think.

I have found I am not alone in this battle to do everything from a place of oneness and fellowship with God, instead of fear. Once, when my husband and I conducted a conference together, this was one of the topics we discussed. Several business people in the audience were particularly intrigued by the practical possibilities of making fellowship with God their prime motivator—not the company incentives plan or their innate fear of failure.

It *is* intriguing. I am increasingly convinced that we as Christians have the choice between two basic motivations for accomplishing anything in life: fear or fellowship. Both fear and its twin sister, anger, are marvelous sources of energy and motivation. However, they are also the Enemy's way of drawing us away from oneness with God, thereby stealing our worship from Him.

Increasingly, I am desirous of living in a way that engages God's heart in fellowship while I am doing my daily tasks. If my strength is coming from worship, communion with God, and confidence in His sufficiency, then I am living as I must live on this earth—I am breathing kingdom air. However, when I catch myself being strengthened and empowered by the fear of what will happen if I don't get some task accomplished, I try to stop myself in midstride and repent of my willingness to be motivated by anything short of communion with Him.

The Bible says, "Whatever you do in word or deed, do all in the name of the Lord Jesus" (Colossians 3:17). I believe this is the mandate for all of the Christian life. Everything we put our hand to can be accomplished from a place of fellowship and fun with God—in His strength and for His glory. Who cares what we accomplish if it has no impact upon God's heart? He will take what we do in our ministry to Him, and from the overflow He'll minister to the earth. Our single mandate is dependence on God and constant fellowship with Him.

Sixteen

BECAUSE YOU LOVE
THE MUSIC

It is so great a thing to be an infinitesimal part
Of this immeasurable orchestra the music
bursts the heart . . .
(From "Instruments" by Madeleine L'Engle)

*I*N CHAPTER 2, I spoke of my cousin Eric and a musical symposium he led at the university near our home. You will recall that Eric was on a brief tour of the Midwestern states and had agreed to lead a master class in trombone while passing through Iowa City. He played some selected pieces and lectured briefly. Let me finish the story of that afternoon.

After Eric's lecture, several students requested that he listen to them play, then critique what he heard. As I listened to the auditions, one young man stands out in my memory. During this student's presentation of the trombone solo from Rimsky-Korsakov's *Russian Easter Overture,* Eric listened attentively. When he finished, Eric asked him to play the piece again.

"Did you know," he asked as the student finished for the second time, "that each time you played the ninth and tenth measures, you rushed through the rests? The part calls for three full beats of rest and you rested only about a beat and a half."

The student reviewed the place on the page where Eric was pointing.

"That oversight could seem trivial," Eric continued, "but it's actually crucial. In fact, in this piece it is disastrous to rush the allotted time of this rest."

Eric looked up at the class.

"You see, during this brief, seemingly unimportant rest, the length of the trombone soloist's silence allows the cello section to be heard making an incredibly beautiful chord change. It is truly a magnificent moment. If the trombone soloist comes in too early, no one will hear the cellos; their moment will pass and the overall beauty of the composition will suffer." Turning back to the student, Eric said, "I want you to find a recording of the *Easter Overture* and listen to it in its entirety over and over until your heart begins to respond to every note. Don't single out the trombone solo; in fact, I want you to be particularly aware of what the string section is doing. Immerse yourself in the piece. Play it in the morning when you get up, during the day as you drive to class, and again at night as you fall asleep. Play it until you can feel it in the deepest part of you and know, without actually hearing it, how it should sound. I want you to learn to love this music—all of it—not just the part that the trombones play.

"If you do this," Eric continued, "if you train your ear to love the whole of this piece, you will be able to play your part with the full sensitivity and impact it requires. Because you love the music, you will not rush through the rests. In fact, because you love the music, you will intuitively play in such a way as to honor and enjoy the other instruments and what each brings to the beauty of the whole.

"Finally, and of equal importance, you won't need to be as concerned about the mechanics of your part. In your desire to preserve the authenticity of what you have come to love, you will begin playing your solo with accuracy. Finding your way into the heart of the composer—learning to hear what he heard, learning to love the piece just as it was written, will give you the ability to play your part with all the sensitivity and impact it deserves."

〜

WHEN JESUS WALKED on the earth, He played His part just as it was written. He came as the Messiah, the God-man who would take away the sins of the world. Though He was King, He took the role of servant; though He was sovereign, He submitted to suffering. He, the Eternal One, took on finite form and purchased with love the allegiance He had every right to require by force.

Because He loved The Music, He did everything precisely as it was written in the Scriptures. Not once did He deviate. Even as He ended His ministry among men and made His way to the cross, Jesus continued in His ministry to His Father by fulfilling every prophetic detail as foretold in the Scriptures. From the act of riding into Jerusalem on the back of a donkey to standing silently before His accusers, He did everything according to plan. He went, as Isaiah had prophesied centuries before, "like a lamb that is led to slaughter" (Isaiah 53:7).

It has always been Jesus' grand passion to do His Father's will and to please His Father's heart. This He did by playing The Music just as it was written. Through the uncompromising obedience of the Son, the glorious music of the Godhead was given full expression all the way to the cross—and beyond.

〜

WE, THE CHURCH, are now the earthly expression of that eternal love song. But if we, like the young university student, are to play The Music with the accuracy and passion it deserves, we must expose our hearts to the constant influence of its beauty and power. By personal, ongoing exposure to all that the Bible says, we will find ourselves responding eagerly to every ageless note, every shift in cadence, every changing chord—every rest. In this way, as we grow in our love for all that is written, several things happen to us simultaneously.

First, we begin to play The Music with the same impact that Jesus' earthly life had. We resonate with the same love Jesus had for His Father as well as for the world He died to save. Our lives begin to have an impact on earth as well as on heaven.

As we learn to carry within us a true, deep love for *all* that has been written, our ministry to God will be much more than an exclusive, ivory-tower interaction with Him alone; it will be a loving, vibrant infiltration of the lives of those around us. By loving what God loves, we will avoid the false, super-spiritual trap of "ministering to God" while selfishly, selectively separating ourselves from what He holds dear. In fact, because of our love for The Music, broken homes and hearts will be touched by its healing refrain; empty, echoing lives will be given a strong new voice, and the salvation song of Jesus will continue to resound in the earth. Guarded by our love for God—and all that He loves—our ministry to Him will remain open, free-flowing, and clearly reflective of His love for the world.

Though our ministry to God does not depend upon human need, for those who love The Music, ministering to God and ministering to humankind are not mutually exclusive activities. Instead, like the skillfully penned notes of a great symphony, they are intricately interwoven.

Second, because we love the Composer and all that He has written, we will rejoice in the part we've been given to play— however great or small. Secure in the ultimate importance of what we've been called to do, we will encourage and applaud the contributions of all those around us.

We will honor every other instrument. Every other person who follows Jesus as Savior and Lord, every other congregation of believers, regardless of denominational affiliation, will be honored in the part they've been given to play. Though we may sound as different from each other as a tuba and a triangle, if we are in the same orchestra, playing with the same genuine love for The Music, the differences will be woven into one whole, harmonic sound.

This we can trust God to do. We can trust Him to conduct what He has composed and to guide what He gave His life for. If we watch Him closely, He will lead us. He will tell each of us when to play and when to rest, when to proceed and when to stop and simply listen—as the cellos make their chord change.

Third, as we minister in this symphony, soon we're not just hearing The Music—we're part of The Music! We're not just reaching for what satisfies our heart, we're entering the celebration of God's heart. From earth we're drawn into the activity of heaven, and a potent, participatory love replaces the lonely longing we once knew. As this love for God and His Music grows, much of what we do as ministry to God comes quite naturally.

In her poem "Instruments," Madeleine L'Engle beautifully captures both the tension and the supreme joy of being a member of the universal body of Christ.

Instruments

Hold me against the dark: I am afraid.
Circle me with your arms. I am made
So tiny and my atoms so unstable
That at any moment I may explode. I am unable

To contain myself in unity. My outlines shiver
With the shock of living. I endeavor
To hold the I as one only for the cloud
Of which I am a fragment, yet to which I'm vowed
To be responsible. Its light against my face
Reveals the witness of the stars, each in its place
Singing, each compassed by the rest,
The many joined to one, the mightiest to the least.
It is so great a thing to be an infinitesimal part
Of this immeasurable orchestra the music bursts the heart,
And from this tiny plosion all the fragments join:
Joy orders the disunity until the song is one.[1]

Because it is joy that orders the disunity among us, our love, our delight in The Music, will draw us into a mutually loving posture in the struggle to become one with each other under the banner of our God who is One.

This joy was evident in a recent e-mail from my cousin.

One of the joys of playing in the Philadelphia Orchestra is the high level of non-verbal communication that goes on, even across such a large group. It is so much fun to participate in that give and take—to hear a beautiful phrase from someone else, and then emulate it when my turn comes. Or, when I happen to stumble upon a beautiful way to interpret my line, to then hear others in the group pick up on what I have just done and continue to expand upon the idea. What we are all trying to do (when things are going their best) is to inspire each other to make music at the highest possible level—to truly arrive at a place where the whole is greater than the sum of its parts.

As Christians who play for love of The Music, we must begin to see each other not as competition, but as inspiring companions, each playing without compromise the salvation song of the Lamb.

Finally, and most importantly, because we love The Music, we will have the courage to follow wherever it may lead. We will have the courage and power to enter the furnace of fellowship and take part in the great exchange of hearts.

Because we love God and The Music He has written, we will have the priestly authority to minister directly to Him. We will become those who carry in our hearts the very heart of the God in whom we delight. No longer will we as mortal men and women seek to be kept safe from His presence. No longer will we cringe in self-protection, for now we are welcomed with great joy and celebration. Jesus said it best in His final declaration to a bewildered world: "It is finished!"[2] The separation is over. The kingdom of heaven is at hand.

So it is that now we come boldly into our communion and walk with assurance into the fire of this fellowship, for Christ has gone before us. No longer do we offer to God our cautious compliance nor bring to Him the feeble praise of a fearful heart. No longer do we rush from His presence into our busyness nor assume a stance of remote interaction.

Instead, carrying within us the confidence and covering of the cross, we joyfully enter the great, ageless exchange of hearts. We are joint heirs with Jesus in the love of His Father! We drink from His cup and partake of His portion! We are bequeathed the treasures of His kingdom and afforded the full rights of His righteousness — the furnace of His fellowship has become our new home!

NOTES

1. THE QUEST

1. *The Constitution of the Presbyterian Church (U.S.A.),* part 1, *Book of Confessions* (Louisville, Ky.: Office of the General Assembly Presbyterian Church [USA], 1999), p. 175.
2. See John 16:33.
3. See Song of Solomon 8:6-7; paraphrase by Brother Hillary, New Melleray Abbey, Dubuque, Iowa.
4. See Genesis 1:26-27.
5. See 1 Peter 2:5.
6. See Deuteronomy 6:4-5; 7:6.
7. See John 4:23; 2 Chronicles 16:9.

2. TO LOVE THE MUSIC

1. Perichoresis (also known in the Latin as *circumincessio)* "means that not only do the three members of the Trinity interpenetrate one another, but all three are involved in all the works of God." The accompanying notion would be that all three Members have complete accessibility to the consciousness and experiences of the others while still maintaining "an element of transcendence, a degree to which each is to be distinguished from the other, allowing the ability to interact with one another as distinct subjects." This is an important distinction because "while total immanence would lead to a Unitarian monotheism, possible of a modalistic type, total transcendence would produce a tritheism of some sort. The combination of both, rather than the exclusion of either

aspect, governs here." Millard J. Erickson, *God in Three Persons: A Contemporary Interpretation of the Trinity* (Grand Rapids, Mich.: Baker, 1995), pp. 225, 235-238.

2. Romans 8:15.
3. Kenneth S. Wuest, *Word Studies In the Greek New Testament,* vol. 2 (Grand Rapids, Mich.: Eerdmans, 1973), p. 95. See "life" in 1 John 1:2. This is *zoe* "as distinguished from bios, physical life, livelihood ..." Spiros Zodhiates, *The Hebrew-Greek Key Study Bible* (Chattanooga, Tenn.: AMG, 1990), p. 1838. The essential truth here is that Christians have been given the life with which God Himself is alive in contrast to the biological life of plants and animals.
4. See 2 Peter 1:4.
5. See Isaiah 56:6-7.
6. See John 15:4-7.
7. See James 2:14-17,24.
8. See Exodus 30:22-38; Mark 12:17; 14:3-9.
9. See John 17:21-26.
10. See Romans 6:7.
11. See Hebrews 3:1; 10:11-23.

3. THE FURNACE OF FELLOWSHIP
1. See Isaiah 6:2.
2. See John 8:58; 10:30; Hebrews 13:8.
3. See Leviticus 10:1.
4. See Acts 2:1-4.
5. See Galatians 4:6-7.
6. See 1 Corinthians 6:19; John 4:21-24.
7. See John 13:34.
8. See 1 Corinthians 3:16; John 4:23.
9. See Romans 12:1.

4. THE FEAR OF FELLOWSHIP

1. See Romans 6:4,11.
2. See Romans 6:5-7.
3. See Galatians 2:20.
4. See Revelation 19:7.
5. See John 15:4-6.

5. PARTAKERS OF THE FLAME

1. See John 17:20-24.
2. See John 14:6.
3. See John 17:20-21.
4. Spiros Zodhiates, ed. *The Hebrew-Greek Key Study Bible* (Chattanooga, Tenn.: AMG, 1990), p. 1841.
5. See Song of Solomon 8:6-7.
6. See 1 Corinthians 13:13.

6. THE WAY IN

1. See Proverbs 8:31.

8. THE GOD WE CAN SEE

1. See Luke 19:1-10.
2. See John 14:6.
3. See 1 Timothy 2:5.
4. See John 10:7,9.
5. See Matthew 11:28; John 6:37.
6. See Luke 5:25.
7. See Luke 7:47-50.
8. See Mark 5:29.
9. Mark 5:30 (NIV).
10. Mark 5:31 (NIV).
11. Mark 5:32 (NIV).
12. See Revelation 3:20.

9. THE REACH OF THE HUNGERING HEART

1. See Job 1:6-12; 2:1-6.

11. FREEDOM TEACHER

1. Helen Keller, *The Story of My Life* (Garden City, N.Y.: Doubleday, 1954), p. 248.
2. Keller, p. 252.
3. Keller, p. 256.
4. See John 15:4.

12. THE COTTAGE

1. Quoted in John Byrom, *Prayer, The Passion of Love* (Oxford, England: SLG Press, 1992), p. 5.
2. Thad Rutter Jr., *Where the Heart Longs to Go* (Nashville, Tenn.: Upper Room Books, 1998), p. 25.
3. Rutter, p.19.
4. John Powell, S.J., *Touched by God* (Allen, Tex.: Thomas More, 1974), p. 33.
5. David B. Biebel, *If God Is So Good, Why Do I Hurt So Bad?* (Grand Rapids, Mich.: Revell, Baker Book House, 1995), p. 61.
6. Rutter, pp. 106, 17.
7. Powell, pp. 23-25.
8. See John 21:12-17.
9. See Hebrews 3:12-19.

13. THE MOMENT OF MEETING

1. Helen Keller, *The Open Door* (Garden City, N.Y.: Doubleday, 1957), p. 136.
2. From Alan Loy McGinnis, *The Friendship Factor* (Minneapolis, Minn.: Augsburg Publishing, 1979), pp. 60-61.
3. See Revelation 8:1.
4. Hebrews 10:15-16.

5. Phillip Yancey, *Disappointment with God* (Grand Rapids, Mich.: Zondervan, 1988), pp. 249-251.

6. Yancey, p. 216.

14. THE SECOND REACH

1. See Philippians 2:10.

15. THE MINDSET OF MINISTERING TO GOD

1. Adapted from Homer, *The Iliad and the Odyssey* (New York: Dorset Press, 1991), p. 68.

2. See 1 Peter 2:6.

3. See John 6:35.

4. See John 5:19,30; 14:31.

5. See Matthew 4:5-11.

16. BECAUSE YOU LOVE THE MUSIC

1. Madeline L'Engle, *The Weather of the Heart* (Wheaton, Ill.: Harold Shaw Publishers, 1978), p. 58.

2. See John 19:30.

ABOUT THE AUTHOR

VICTORIA BROOKS and her husband, Dr. Michael Brooks, live in Cedar Rapids, Iowa, with their three sons, Nathan, Jordan, and Zion.

Vicki was born in Quito, Ecuador, the daughter of missionaries Dick and Jody Larson, and the granddaughter of Reuben and Grace Larson, cofounders of pioneer missionary radio station HCJB: The Voice of the Andes.

After spending her early years in Quito and in Lima, Peru, Vicki returned to the United States with her parents when she was four. She grew up in Wheaton, Illinois, and attended Covenant College in Lookout Mountain, Tennessee, and Wheaton College, and studied psychology at Northern Illinois University.

She spent five years as a counselor in the Illinois Department of Corrections, working at two maximum-security state facilities for male felony offenders.

She is the author of *Ministering to God: The Reach of the Heart* and has challenged Christians in the United States and abroad with the biblical call to minister *to* God not just *for* God. She carries a message of personal hope for all Christians who find the tasks and demands of everyday life crowding out the intimacy and immediacy of their relationship with God.

Vicki gives both scriptural and practical methods for sustaining a personal ministry to God while remaining faithful to the earthly work and ministry God has given each of us to do.

DO YOU KNOW HOW TO ENJOY THE CHRISTIAN LIFE?

Intimacy with God
Getting to know someone is hard enough,
but it's even harder when they can't be seen or touched.
This study gives readers a chance to really know God—His
character, personality, and relevancy to everyday life—through
the power and passion of the Psalms.
(Cynthia Heald)

When God Whispers
This collection of insightful Scripture-based meditations will
encourage you and remind you of God's extraordinary love
He reveals to us, even in the midst of ordinary days.
(Carole Mayhall)

When the Soul Listens
Feeling as if God isn't speaking to you? Build a lasting
connection with God as you discover spiritual direction
that will lead you to rest and guidance in Him.
(Jan Johnson)

Pleasures Evermore
Falling in love with Jesus, rather than following a list of rules,
is the foundation for holiness. Discover the joy of fulfilling your
deepest desires through a commitment to true godliness.
(Sam Storms)

To get your copies, visit your local bookstore, call 1-800-366-7788,
or log on to www.navpress.com. Ask for a FREE catalog of
NavPress products. Offer #BPA.

NAVPRESS
BRINGING TRUTH TO LIFE
www.navpress.com